"Julie de Azevedo Hanks has ⬚ ⬚h-needed and long-awaited resource for self-expression. Her compassionate and informative voice gently guides readers through potential obstacles with hands-on strategies, which are validating and empowering. *The Assertiveness Guide for Women* is a must-read for anyone seeking the support and tools essential for honest and healthy communication."

> —**Karen Kleiman, MSW**, founder of The Postpartum Stress Center, and author of several books on postpartum depression, including *Therapy and the Postpartum Woman*

"*The Assertiveness Guide for Women* offers the skills you need to change and empower your life—including strengthening valuable relationships! Julie de Azevedo Hanks' down-to-earth, warm style invites you in and shows you you're not alone, as she provides a foundation of emotional awareness, understanding, and confidence to enable you to express your truest self. A powerful tool for women of all ages and stages, this book can, and if followed, *will* change you for the best!"

> —**Christina G. Hibbert, PsyD**, author of *This is How We Grow, Who Am I Without You?*, and *8 Keys to Mental Health Through Exercise*

"*The Assertiveness Guide for Women* provides helpful exercises and tools that will help any woman find her authentic voice. Julie de Azevedo Hanks helps readers identify the barriers that get in the way of assertive communication, and then provides the action steps necessary for achieving healthy self-expression."

> —**Amy Morin, LCSW**, author of *13 Things Mentally Strong People Don't Do*

"So many of us have experiences of silencing ourselves—sometimes for years and years. *The Assertiveness Guide for Women* is a powerful book packed with practical, thoughtful suggestions and poignant real-life examples to help us speak up, effectively express ourselves, and set strong boundaries. You'll also gain insights into your own thoughts, feelings, and relationships, and into your own challenges with being assertive. This book empowers you, even when you feel powerless and undeserving. I truly wish it was required reading for all women and girls. It's that important."

—**Margarita Tartakovsky, MS**, writer and associate
editor at www.psychcentral.com

"This informative, accessible guide goes beyond healthy communication techniques and delves into the psychology that drives our patterns of relating to others. With thorough information, relatable examples, and awareness exercises that personalize the experience, Julie de Azevedo Hanks provides readers with a highly applicable resource that can transform their relationships with others and with themselves. In a society that makes assertiveness challenging for many women, this book can be a life-changer."

—**Elizabeth Anne Scott, MS**, author of 8 *Keys to*
*Stress Management*

THE
# ASSERTIVENESS
# GUIDE
*for*
# Women

—— HOW TO ——
COMMUNICATE YOUR NEEDS,
SET HEALTHY BOUNDARIES &
TRANSFORM YOUR RELATIONSHIPS


JULIE DE AZEVEDO HANKS, PhD


New Harbinger Publications, Inc.

## Publisher's Note

Distributed in Canada by Raincoast Books

Copyright © 2016 by Julie de Azevedo Hanks
     New Harbinger Publications, Inc.
     5674 Shattuck Avenue
     Oakland, CA 94609
     www.newharbinger.com

Cover design by Amy Shoup
Interior design by Michele Waters-Kermes
Acquired by Melissa Valentine
Edited by Marisa Solís

### Library of Congress Cataloging-in-Publication Data

Names: De Azevedo, Julie, author.

Title: The assertiveness guide for women : how to communicate your needs, set healthy boundaries, and transform your relationships / Julie de Azevedo Hanks ; foreword by Riane Eisler.

Description: Oakland, CA : New Harbinger Publications, [2016] | Includes bibliographical references.

Identifiers: LCCN 2016015122 (print) | LCCN 2016023998 (ebook) | ISBN 9781626253377 (paperback) | ISBN 9781626253384 (pdf e-book) | ISBN 9781626253391 (epub) | ISBN 9781626253384 (PDF e-book) | ISBN 9781626253391 (ePub)

Subjects: LCSH: Assertiveness in women. | Assertiveness (Psychology) | Self-confidence. | Interpersonal communication. | Interpersonal relations. | BISAC: PSYCHOLOGY / Interpersonal Relations. | SELF-HELP / Personal Growth / Self-Esteem.

Classification: LCC BF575.A85 D42 2016 (print) | LCC BF575.A85 (ebook) | DDC 158.2082--dc23

LC record available at https://lccn.loc.gov/2016015122

Printed in the United States of America.

23  23  21

10  9  8  7

To Madeline and Macy: May you always be the main characters in your lives. Your voices matter...

# Contents

# Foreword

I wish I could have had this book years ago when, along with thousands of other women, I suddenly woke up, as if from a long drugged sleep, and began to question conventional ideas about what is—and is not—"feminine."

That was in 1969, and many things have changed since then. We got rid of some blatantly discriminatory laws, transformed want ads so they were not segregated into "help wanted male" and "help wanted female" (the latter consisting of dead-end "helper" jobs), and managed to get legislation aimed at protecting girls and women from violence, including beatings at home, which were then pretty much ignored.

But far too much remains the same. Workplaces are still generally based on a "masculine" model whereby there is little or no paid parental leave. Political leadership remains a largely male preserve. And many of us are still brought up to take care of others, even if it is at the expense of taking care of ourselves—for which we pay a high price emotionally, physically, and economically.

Over the years, I have written extensively about women in various legal and cultural contexts. My first books, including *The Equal Rights Handbook*, drew largely from my legal background. Then, in *The Chalice and the Blade* and subsequent publications, I focused on the cultural and historical barriers to women's empowerment, and what is needed to overcome them.

And now my compendium of writings includes this foreword, because it's for a book that complements works written by and for women for the betterment of women. *The Assertiveness Guide for Women: How to Communicate Your Needs, Set Healthy Boundaries, and Transform Your Relationships* provides a much-needed step-by-step guide for empowering women. At its core is building healthy relationships, starting with how we relate to ourselves.

Julie de Azevedo Hanks draws on her experience as a psychotherapist and clinical social worker, as well as extensive research, to show us how to cut through our gender socialization and move past behavioral and relational patterns to find and express our own voices. But at the same time that she provides us with tools for self-empowerment, she shows how we can do this without disempowering others. This is one of many things that makes this book special.

Another unique feature is that it does not look at our individual lives in isolation but in the context of both our personal network of relations and our larger culture. Still another is that, rather than steering women toward simply adopting more traditionally "masculine" roles, it recognizes the enormous importance of the traditional "women's work" of care, redefining it as human work that both men and women can and must do, including not only caring for others but also caring for oneself. Most important, it provides practical, easy-to-use tools for making the necessary changes to implement all this in our day-to-day lives.

Julie has developed a powerful method for helping us understand our particular attachment styles and how becoming aware of them can free us from patterns that hold us back. She shares effective tools for self-soothing and self-compassion.

Julie is a gifted storyteller, which makes this book all the more special. I was particularly moved by her accounts of personal transformations—her own and those of her clients. These are powerful stories told with compassion and warmth in ways that touch our hearts.

I first met Julie when she enrolled in my online course "Changing Our Stories, Changing Our Lives: From Domination to Partnership." I was impressed by her participation in the course, and even more so when she immediately put what we covered into action by launching her own program: her Partnership Model of Family Organization on how to transform families so everyone can realize her or his potential without being imprisoned in traditional gender roles.

Later, when Julie obtained her Caring Economy Advocate certificate from the Center for Partnership Studies, I was again impressed by her deep understanding of and commitment to changing the devaluation of women and the "feminine." I was also moved by her passion and caring—qualities that shine through every page of this book, as does her dedication to using her many gifts to help others.

*The Assertiveness Guide for Women* shows how we can develop the skills to make our needs and feelings known and set boundaries, while also being sensitive to the needs and feelings of others. This is key to the partnership model of relations that Julie deeply understands and applies—and is an important way that this book is different from other assertiveness guides.

This focus on our human need for caring connection is at the heart of this book. At the same time, the guidelines and exercises Julie provides in each chapter are easy to grasp and apply to our own lives.

I am convinced that this book will be enormously helpful to all its readers and that they, in turn, will be able to use it to help others. You have an exciting journey ahead of you as you read, enjoy, and use this wonderful book!

—Riane Eisler, JD, PhD (Hon.)
Author of *The Chalice and the Blade* and
*The Real Wealth of Nations*
January 2016

# Introduction

As human beings, we have an ingrained desire to make meaningful connections with each other and form enduring bonds. It's been said that our very survival is dependent on healthy, nurturing, and secure relationships. How do we form quality connections to others? Decades of research conclude that communication is a major factor. But as we all know, there are many ways to communicate, and some are more effective than others. So is there a magic formula? No. Is there a magic wand? Nope. But there *are* specific skills that you can develop and practice that are key to creating healthier relationships. And it begins with *assertiveness*.

So what is assertiveness? If you've picked up this book, you likely have some idea of what assertiveness means—because you think you don't have it, or don't have enough of it, or find it hard to use it when you need to. All of us have difficulty at one time or another with asserting ourselves—at work, with family members, with our significant others. Some of us need occasional help being assertive in critical meetings or when our children are particularly challenging. Others experience difficulty with assertiveness so often that we feel like no one ever hears us or understands us on a daily basis. No matter where you fall on the spectrum, this book can help!

Assertiveness is generally defined as a way of communicating that is clear, confident, and self-assured. It enables you to express your thoughts, feelings, needs, and wants without infringing on the rights of others. Assertiveness skills help you articulate your unique sense of self while maintaining your connection with others and allowing them to have an experience that is different from yours. At its core, assertiveness is about the courage to express *difference*.

While this book is titled an *assertiveness guide*, it's really about much more. It's about deepening your understanding of yourself and what makes you tick. It's about looking at how you relate to people—from the attachments made when you were a child to your current relationships as an adult—and making sense of the many communication styles you've likely encountered. This book will teach you how to develop emotional awareness and to allow your feelings to guide you but not overwhelm you. You will gain the tools to effectively expand beyond unhelpful communication patterns. You'll learn tips on what to say, how to say it, and when to say it so that your message gets across. When you can stand up for yourself, you can transform your relationships!

Experiencing difficulties with assertiveness is certainly not gender specific. However, from my graduate studies and my clinical and personal experience, I have come to believe that women have some unique challenges when it comes to taking a stand and speaking up for themselves and for others. Girls are generally socialized to be nice, compliant, and relationship-oriented, while boys are often socialized to be independent and strong, and they're encouraged to speak up. Girls and boys are treated differently in families and educational settings in ways that frequently discourage girls from having and expressing strong emotions and opinions. Societal expectations have historically taught women that they should, above all, take care of others and be self-sacrificing. While these cooperative ideals are vital for families and communities to flourish, if not balanced with permission to assert thoughts, feelings, wants, and needs, these expectations can become barriers to a woman's ability to express herself, create intimate relationships, experience personal effectiveness, and have emotional health and well-being.

Although this book focuses primarily on what women can do on an individual level to learn and implement change in their own lives, it is not my intent to minimize the pervasive societal factors that often leave women feeling minimized and powerless to assert themselves. The larger systemic problems of income inequality, high poverty rates among women and children, rigidity of gender role expectations, and institutionalized violence against women play a *large* part in shaping the experiences of women, both as individuals and as a group, when it comes to gender and assertiveness. All too often, women have needed to silence themselves in order to survive, or at least to not worsen their situation. Although these gender inequalities are real and powerful, they are not the focus of this self-help guide.

The primary focus of this book is sharing what women themselves can learn and do to make it more likely that their feelings, thoughts, needs, and wants will be heard and responded to in positive ways. By developing awareness of relationship styles (also referred to as "attachment styles" in this book), enhancing awareness and management of emotions, and learning viable skills to put assertiveness into practice, you can empower yourself and get your needs met—while simultaneously developing empathy for, sensitivity to, and validation of the experiences of those around you.

## Why This Book?

Three primary things make this book different from other books on assertiveness: First, it is specifically written for women by a woman, and second, I use a more encompassing definition of "assertiveness" that involves not only the clear communication piece but also how to know what you feel, think, want, and need in the first place! I focus on relationships dynamics in this book because assertive communication doesn't happen in a vacuum—it takes at least two to communicate! This book will help you gain a deeper awareness of yourself *and* your relationships. As a result, you will learn to be a better communicator *and* improve the bonds of those with whom you associate.

The third element that makes this book stand out from others is that it comes from both a personal and professional place. I have personally experienced the struggle to be assertive and express my feelings, thoughts, needs, and wants. It took several years for me to develop a deep awareness of my internal experiences, to accept my differences, and to gain the skills to effectively communicate them in my relationships. This realization materialized out of sessions with a counselor when I was a teenager. Our talks were life-changing and opened up a new way of viewing the world; I finally started to understand some deeper sources of my pain, and I learned skills to help identify and manage my emotions. It was this experience that inspired my future career choice as a therapist; I wanted to help others have the same emotional insight and personal transformation that I gained, along with the positive changes and sense of empowerment that I had experienced.

In my first few years of college, I was introduced to the concept of *attachment:* how we are wired to connect with other human beings in order to survive—emotionally and physically—and how we develop a default relationship template based on our interaction with our primary caregivers. These early attachments inform our senses of self and safety, our expectations in future relationships, and how we manage emotions. In other words, our early attachment styles inform our emotional development—our core beliefs about ourselves and the world—and create a template of what we can expect in future relationships.

In my twenty-plus years of clinical practice as a psychotherapist I have witnessed firsthand the pain and frustration of many women who felt they were unable to be assertive—that is, to identify their feelings and thoughts, needs and wants; to make clear and strong requests of others; and to set strong boundaries in their relationships. I have seen the damaging consequences of women not being willing (due to a sense of poor self-worth), not being able (due to lack of knowledge and skills), or not feeling safe enough (due to gender socialization, past relationships patterns, and current relationship choices) in their relationships to act assertively and create the life they want.

It has been more than thirty years since I sat in my first therapy session as the *client*. Since then, I have continued to learn more about the connection among attachment, emotions, and assertiveness through graduate school studies, clinical practice, attending therapy myself, readings, and professional trainings. The skills presented in this book really work—they have worked for me personally and also for hundreds of my clients. By learning these concepts and skills, I have been able to be far more effective in all aspects of my life, particularly in developing a deep sense self-worth, creating and maintaining satisfying relationships, and in achieving my professional aspirations. Although my name is on the cover of this book as an "expert," I view myself as a fellow journeywoman trying to untangle the complexities of life, emotions, and relationships while continuing on a path of growth.

# How This Book Will Help You

Learning how and when to be assertive will bring more joy and fulfillment in your relationships with others, as well as peace and confidence within yourself. Period. If you are willing to do the numerous exercises in this book and practice the skills herein, I promise you will develop a greater sense of:

- *Clarity* about yourself and others through *self-reflection*—the ability to reflect on your history to understand your current patterns

- *Confidence* through *self-awareness*—the ability to identify your feelings, thoughts, needs, and wants

- *Calmness* of mind/heart/body through *self-soothing*—the ability to calm yourself down so you can access your awareness and communication skills

- *Connection* through your *self-expression*—the ability to clearly communicate and make requests, and to take action so you can speak and act confidently and congruently in ways that will improve your relationships

- *Compassion* for others whose experiences differ from yours by inviting *self-expansion*—the ability to stand firmly on your own two feet while "holding the lantern" that illuminates a situation, or holds space for another person's view, even when it's different from yours

Chapter 1 introduces my definition of assertiveness as a willingness and ability to express your feelings, thoughts, needs, and wants—even when they differ from those around you. This chapter also outlines the five aspects of assertiveness.

Then we'll move on in chapter 2 to explore the roots of *attachment theory* and the three basic attachment styles, discuss the idea of *differentiation*, and consider how attachment and differentiation relate to your assertiveness challenges.

In chapter 3, we'll take a brief look at some of the family and societal influences that have worked against women finding and using their voices. We'll then move on in chapter 4 to self-reflection and exploring your past relationship history and relationship patterns.

Next, chapter 5 focuses on self-awareness, particularly on identifying and naming your feelings, and developing emotional intelligence. Building on the idea of emotions, chapter 6 outlines specific self-soothing and emotion management strategies to help you calm yourself down during intense situations so you can communicate more effectively.

Chapters 7 and 8 center on self-expression by outlining the three stances of communication—the Doormat, the Sword, and the Lantern. Self-expression skills are introduced, including how to focus on setting strong boundaries and how to reclaim your right to say no. Also offered are simple formulas for assertive communication, making requests, and incorporating compassion in your communication—all with the objective of increasing the likelihood that your assertiveness will be heard and understood.

Finally, in chapter 9 we'll go into detail about self-expansion, the Lantern stance, and ways to illuminate difficult situations and assert yourself. I'll also tie together how the skills in this book will lead to more *clarity, confidence, calmness, connection,* and *compassion*—characteristics that will enable you to transform your life. I'll bring it all together and then offer additional resources to help you on your journey of growth.

The goal of this assertiveness guide is to encourage you to look back, tune in, and then learn to speak up in your relationships in such a way that you can create authentic connections with others and transform aspects of your life that have left you feeling dissatisfied. My objective is for you to view yourself as a self-aware, powerful, and effective communicator in personal and work relationships by understanding what assertiveness is, what barriers are in the way to your speaking up, what your emotions and attachment style are, and how to confidently share your differences in ways that can strengthen your relationships.

The bonds of relationships are a perfect way to conclude this introduction because they represent our core need as human beings: to feel connected to ourselves and to each other. I hope that this book helps you on your path of discovery and growth to improve your understanding of yourself and your relationship patterns. I hope the skills you learn will improve your personal well-being and enrich your ties to others. "Being the 'best you can be' is really only possible when you are deeply connected to another. Splendid isolation is for planets, not people" (Johnson, 2013).

# What Does It Mean to Be Assertive?

"I'm always the one who is accommodating or apologizing!" said Anna as she choked on her tears. "And I'm tired of it. What about me? What about what *I* want? When am *I* going to matter in my own life?" Anna, a working mother of two teens and wife of eighteen years, had come to therapy to address feelings of chronic unhappiness and lack of energy. When I asked her how she felt about her life, what was missing, and what she wanted to create for herself, she paused and looked down, contemplating the question. After a long silence, she looked up at me through puzzled, teary-eyed, and quietly said, "I have no idea. I'm so busy trying to keep everyone else happy that I've never stopped to ask myself that."

Jenna, a single woman in her twenties who works long hours at a law firm, sat down in my office, exasperated. She sought psychotherapy due to an increase in worry and anxiety, sleeplessness, and work-related stress. "My boss expects me to work 24/7. I am so sick of it. She e-mails me, texts me, and calls my

cell even when I'm supposed to be off the clock. She even inter-
rupted me when I was on a date last weekend with a stupid
question about a case I'm working on. Can't she wait until
Monday? Doesn't she know I have a *life?* I am feeling burned out
and stuck in this job, but I can't afford to quit."

During my two decades in clinical practice, I have worked
with hundreds of women from many walks of life who had
become overwhelmed and resentful after perceiving that they
had been dismissed, unheard, undervalued, or overlooked in
their important relationships. Whether with a romantic partner,
family member, friend, child, neighbor, boss, or coworker, many
women struggle to know how to identify and share their feelings, thoughts, wants, and needs in clear and productive ways
that allow their needs to be met *and* their relationships with
others to be preserved. Because assertiveness is an expression of
difference (there's no real need to be assertive if our thoughts
and feelings are in perfect unison with someone else, right?), it
is common for women to fear that these differences will create
problems or distance in the relationship.

However, my career and life experiences have taught me
that the opposite is usually true: Clearly communicating my
feelings, thoughts, needs, and wants—and then really claiming
and valuing them as *my own*—is one of the most effective ways
to strengthen relationships, build confidence, and create the
life I want. The more secure I am with myself, the more I can
experience true intimacy with others. And the same can be
true for you! I believe that with a little more insight into your
*attachment style,* or relationship template; an understanding of
how to identify and use emotions in healthy ways; and a handful
of practical tools to help you gain self-awareness, you will be
more comfortable being assertive in all of your relationships.

What do I mean by *assertiveness?* For some, it might suggest
saying whatever is on your mind; telling people off; being rude,

abrasive, or thoughtless; or being indifferent or inconsiderate. Others may associate assertiveness with discussions underscored by highly escalated emotions, giving the cold shoulder, or even verbal fights and door slamming. Assertiveness is clearly a loaded word that has different shades of meaning.

I surveyed an anonymous group of 280 women on how they define assertiveness. Here are a variety of responses in their own words:

- *The ability to make your needs and desires known, and to defend yourself in an appropriate manner*

- *The ability to say no, mean no, and follow through on the no*

- *Having the confidence and courage to be your own advocate*

- *Being able to present one's point of view without being timid or aggressive*

- *Being bold and confident, standing up for yourself or others, and expressing your thoughts, ideas, and concerns*

## AWARENESS EXERCISE
### How Do You Define Assertiveness?

Consider the following questions:

- Think about the word "assertiveness." What thoughts and images arise in your mind when you ponder this word?

- How do you choose to define assertiveness in your own life?

- Do you consider yourself to be an assertive person?

A downloadable worksheet for this exercise—and the other awareness exercises in this book—is available at **http://www .newharbinger.com/33377**.

From the many answers given in my survey, a commonality emerged: women associate assertiveness with confidence, the ability to communicate, and a move toward action. By the time you are done with this book, I want you to view yourself as an assertive woman.

## Five Skills of Assertiveness

For the purposes of this book, I define assertiveness as having the following five skills (the 5 S's) and five positive results (the 5 C's):

1. **Self-Reflection:** An understanding of your attachment style, differentiation level, and relationship patterns. The result of self-reflection is a sense of *clarity* about your own development, your relationship patterns, and how your past is impacting your ability to be assertive.

2. **Self-Awareness:** An awareness of your feelings, thoughts, needs, and wants resulting in a sense of *confidence* about what you want to communicate.

3. **Self-Soothing:** The ability to manage your intense emotions and employ skills to soothe yourself and respond to emotions in a caring way, without becoming overwhelmed by them or detaching from them. The development of self-soothing leads to a sense of *calmness*, which allows you to clearly assert yourself and convey your intended message.

4. **Self-Expression:** The ability to communicate your feelings, thoughts, needs, and wants clearly to others, along with a willingness to back up your words with action. The development of skills to express yourself leads to a stronger and deeper *connection* with others.

5. **Self-Expansion:** The openness to another's point of view as being valid, the willingness to "hold space" for differences, and the desire to grow through your relationships. The practice of hearing and valuing another's experience leads to deeper feelings of *compassion* for another's experience.

A downloadable list of the Five Skills of Assertiveness is available at **http://www.newharbinger.com/33377**.

Now let's explore each of these assertiveness skills in a little more depth, shall we?

## Self-Reflection

Self-reflection includes an understanding of how past attachment styles and relationship patterns are impacting your current relationships and your approach to assertive communication. As you develop an understanding of and an appreciation for your own attachment style, differentiation level, and relationship template, you will be more effective at developing the skills to overcome barriers to assertive communication. In the coming chapters we'll explore your attachment style and examine how it may be supporting or sabotaging your ability to assert yourself clearly and effectively in your life right now. Here's an example:

Ella came into my office for therapy. She was well dressed and communicated in a very formal manner. Ella informed me that she was there to talk about sex, which she didn't enjoy. She dreaded her husband's flirtations and innuendos because they were a prelude to Lonnie asking her for sex. She felt guilty and ashamed, and also angry that he pressured her. For more than fifteen years Ella had resented her relationship with her Lonnie because she believed that he wanted her to be skinnier, sexier, and more adventurous in bed than she was or wanted to be.

When I asked about their first sexual relationship, she reluctantly shared how scary it was. She had married young and with no prior sexual experiences. Her husband, on the other hand, had had sexual experiences with previous girlfriends in high school and college. Ella explained, "He knew a lot more than I did about sex, and it was overwhelming to me." It was rare that they talked openly about their sexual relationship or about anything touchy. When they did, it quickly turned into a fight about who was to blame for their strained relationship or days of cold silence between them. "It's just better not to talk about it," Ella said.

Taking a step back from her current concerns, Ella explained some of her family history. Her parents had a tumultuous marriage, fighting loudly and often. Her mother was very critical of Ella, even though she tried desperately to please her by being pretty, getting good grades, and being helpful around the house.

*All those things I did—it was never enough for my mom. Even to this day, when I share something I'm excited about, she'll come back with something negative.*

*My parents often fought in front of me, but even if I wasn't in the room I could still hear the horrible and hateful things they'd scream at each other. I never really felt safe in my own house, and I had no one to help me through it, no one to comfort me. The people who were supposed to protect me were the ones whose behavior was hurting me.*

Ella started to connect the dots.

*I don't feel safe with Lonnie, just like I never felt safe with my parents or good enough for my mom! When my mom started being critical, I would tune her out and then try even harder to please her. That's what I do now, with Lonnie. I've never noticed that before. I listen to him, but I don't really take in what he's saying. It's just too painful, too critical, too familiar. But then, as I replay his words in my mind, I end up trying to do more and do better—to be a better mother, be more organized at home, be more attractive—and to be happier.*

I asked Ella if she'd ever told her mother how painful her criticisms were, or if she'd made any requests to end the critical comments. Ella hadn't. Then I asked if she had ever shared with Lonnie how overwhelmed she was during the beginning of their marriage by her lack of sexual experience and knowledge, and how his requests to do things that she didn't want to do—and his criticism of her being frigid, prude, and chubby— really hurt her. She hadn't done that either; she'd never developed the skills or the emotional safety in her marriage to make her feelings known.

Ella's early family relationship was clearly playing out in her current life. She had developed an avoidant style of relating to her parents as a way to protect herself from the instability and negativity, and she was relating in a similar way with her husband. She had learned to let people talk, to tune them out, and then try harder to be "good"—a good daughter and then a good wife and mother.

Through therapy, she continued to hone her ability to reflect on and to understand the relationship and communication patterns she had developed in her early life—and how she had continued using them as an adult. Most important, she was able to grieve the nurturing and safety she didn't have as a child, as well as the years lost to a strained marriage. Through *self-reflection*, Ella developed a sense of *clarity* about how her past experiences and patterns were impacting her current relationship. She began to see why it was difficult for her to share her feelings, thoughts, needs, and wants in her marriage.

## Self-Awareness

In order to express yourself assertively and effectively to others, you need to develop deeper self-awareness by learning how to tune in to what you feel, what you think, what you need, and what you want. An important step in developing assertiveness skills is to become mindful of what's going on inside of you—in your mind, your heart, and your body. Self-awareness is the foundation of assertive communication and strong relationships; *you* have to know what you're experiencing before you can express yourself to someone else and be heard!

Awareness of your feelings, thoughts, needs, and wants allows you to create mutually fulfilling relationships with the people who matter most to you. When you lack self-awareness or withhold information that you *are* aware of from your loved ones, you not only restrict your own growth but theirs as well (Miller and Stiver 1997). People grow in and through relationships.

The following example from another client illustrates how the awareness of emotions, thoughts, needs, and wants develops the confidence to know when you need to speak up and what to ask for in ways that maintain the relationship:

> *I have been asking my boss for more work hours for quite a while now. Not only has he not given them to me, he repeatedly schedules me to work weekends, even though I've also expressed that I need weekends off sometimes. Things got worse when a new girl got more hours than me but didn't have to work weekends. I was so upset that I finally directly confronted my boss and clearly asked for what I wanted. He admitted that he needed to take another look at the schedule and make some changes. I was afraid he might think I was being a bitch, but I knew I had a valid point that needed to be addressed.*

The more *aware* you are of your internal cues, the more *confident* you feel, and the greater ability you have to manage your emotions and effectively communicate. As you learn about attachment styles in the coming chapters, you'll see that each style has unique challenges when it comes to tuning in to emotions, thoughts, needs, and wants. Each style also has different obstacles when it comes to speaking and acting assertively.

## Self-Soothing

One of the great things about relationships is having someone who can give support and love in times of grief, crisis, or pain. There's something remarkably comforting about crying on a friend's shoulder (figuratively or literally) and knowing that someone cares about you when you are troubled or sad. It is also an important skill for you to turn inward to seek help—that is, to rely on yourself to provide comfort and calm yourself down. This is where self-soothing comes in.

Self-soothing is the ability to manage your own emotions in difficult or stressful situations without being overwhelmed by them or denying them. What this means is that it's necessary to tune in to what you're feeling—but not to the point that your emotions are essentially controlling you. Assertiveness comes from a place of emotional awareness but not emotional volatility.

When you feel threatened with loss, rejection, or disconnection, you may become emotionally "flooded." When experiencing intense emotions, your prefrontal cortex (the part of your brain responsible for abstract thinking and analyzing and regulating your behavior) gets hijacked by your "primitive brain" (brain stem). Your primitive brain is designed to help you survive in life-threatening situations. When you perceive a threat (physical, relational, or emotional), your brain goes into survival mode, also referred to as the fight, flight, or freeze response. Being able to calm *yourself* down allows you to access the self-reflection, self-awareness, and communication skills that you will develop throughout this book.

According to stress researcher and biologist Dr. Robert Sapolsky (2004), animals are much better at managing threats to their well-being than humans. Animals go into a temporary survival mode for only a few minutes while they run from or fight off their predator. If they survive, their bodies go back into homeostasis, and their fight, flight, or freeze response turns off. While humans do occasionally have to respond to external threats to survival in cases of accidents, natural disasters, and violence, the vast majority of threats we face is psychological in nature and originates not from outside us but from our own thoughts. Feeling nervousness about losing a job, stress about finances, pressure about a deadline, or anxiety about asserting yourself in an important relationship are just a few examples of common human experiences that can activate stress hormones in the brain. Because the body reacts to these stressors as if it were in physical danger, those who have strong emotional responses to these triggers (which can be daily!) suffer greatly. Being able to self-soothe becomes a necessary antidote.

Unfortunately, we cannot simply turn off our responses in the same way that animals can, thus making humans quite unique in our experience of chronic stress. Because we are not biologically wired to physically and emotionally relax following a distressing situation, we must learn and practice strategies to help ourselves to once again be calm.

Sandra worked full-time as an assistant in a law firm and was studying late one night for the bar exam. By the time she went to bed it was around 1:00 a.m. Here is how the night progressed:

*My neighbor in the apartment next to me had his TV up so loud that I couldn't sleep! It sounded like some kind of violent action flick. As I tossed and turned, I got more and more angry that someone would be so insensitive and selfish and have such a lack of respect for others' needs. I started thinking about banging on his door and screaming in his face that he was a selfish bastard who had no regard for others and that I was going to call the cops if he didn't turn down his TV.*

*This neighbor was an acquaintance and was generally not disruptive. But the more I started visualizing telling him off, the more angry I felt. A hot burning sensation was rising in my body, and I could feel the muscles in my shoulders, arms, and hands tense up. I knew that if I continued with these thoughts and down this emotional path the outcome would not be good—for either of us. So I sat up in bed, closed my eyes, took a couple of deep breaths, and started practicing self-compassion, which I've been working on in therapy. "Of course you're angry," I said to myself as I gently stroked my arm. "You're under extreme stress right now. You've worked hard and studied hard and you just want some sleep. Of course you're upset by your neighbor's insensitivity preventing you from getting what you need right now."*

*I could feel my heart rate going down and my muscles relaxing. Then I started to make a plan about how to assert myself so I could get some rest. I put on some sweats and walked next door and knocked loudly on the door—not pissed-off knocking but loud enough that he could hear it. He opened the door with a puzzled look on his face. I said in a firm yet kind voice, "Hey, Scott, it's been a rough day for me. Will you turn your TV volume down? I can hear it through the wall and it's preventing me from falling asleep." He said he was so sorry and didn't realize how late it was. He turned down the volume on the TV, and I fell asleep.*

Sandra's response to the neighbor's noisiness is certainly understandable. She was exhausted and stressed and went into "fight" mode. Through self-soothing, she was able to access her higher-level thinking and come up with a plan that would help Sandra to get her needs met and to preserve the relationship with her neighbor. Had she gone over to his apartment in fight mode she would likely have experienced a much different and less-than-positive outcome.

On the other extreme of the emotional response spectrum are individuals who have limited or no access to their emotional experiences. Perhaps they aren't fully conscious of them, learn to numb them, or simply ignore what they're feeling. This state could be thought of as an emotional shutdown or emotional numbness. I believe that one of the main reasons people avoid emotions is because they don't know how to manage them, particularly if they are difficult, uncomfortable, or overwhelming. While this coping strategy may (temporarily) shield you from pain, this approach doesn't allow you to be fully connected to yourself; it impedes your ability to act assertively and create meaningful relationships. Emotional management skills can help you first access and then soothe emotions. The development of *self-soothing* skills allows you to move toward *calmness* so you can access your higher brain and express yourself in a clear and congruent way.

In the next chapter, we'll explore in more depth why our survival responses get activated so often in response to real or perceived threats to our relationships when I talk about attachment styles.

## Self-Expression

As you practice tuning in and use different strategies to manage the intensity of emotions that arise, the next step is to develop and implement the skills necessary to express yourself clearly and effectively (which will then increase the likelihood that your message will be well received and responded to). The following is an example of a woman who successfully expressed an emotional need:

> *I recently told my partner that I needed more uninterrupted attention from her. She said she was grateful to know what I needed so she wouldn't have to guess. I feel proud and empowered that I was able to communicate this to her. And since that time, our pattern of being too busy for each other has improved.*

Asking for what you want and need is what being assertive is all about! In this example, her partner was grateful for a direct request. But as you've probably already experienced, not everyone will feel grateful when you're assertive. You will likely get a variety of responses as you start speaking up more frequently. Keep in mind that assertiveness skills aren't about pleasing other people or about elevating yourself above others. Assertiveness is about treating yourself as an equal with others, and taking ownership of your well-being while respecting others' differences.

Though it might seem counterintuitive, the closer a person is to you emotionally, the harder it may be to assert yourself to him or her when a difference arises, especially when it comes to vulnerable emotions like fear and loneliness. For example, it's easy to become frustrated, even enraged, at an individual who cuts you off in traffic or is driving carelessly; you might even make a corrective or demeaning gesture. However, it can be more difficult to speak up assertively when the individual driving too fast, weaving through traffic, or disobeying the rules of the road is your spouse (you might find it easier to act passively and say nothing, or you might communicate aggressively and say something like, "Ugh! I hate riding in a car with you! You're going to kill us!"—both of which are examples of *not* acting assertively).

For another example, consider how the digital age has changed communication etiquette. While the Internet can be a wonderful place to learn and exchange ideas, unfortunately it can also be quite a nasty outlet for trolls, or people determined to express their views in a manner that is less than civil. I do my best to avoid negative, hateful comment sections for articles posted online, but I have seen enough of them to understand that there are some vicious responses to cultural and social issues. The most negative things I've seen online are, not surprising, by people named "anonymous" (or those using an obvious alias). These folks don't have anything to lose by being mean or hateful because they have *no* investment in the relationship with the person they are targeting.

I find it helpful to consider levels of relationships as concentric circles. You are the center of the circle. Those closest to you (such as your spouse, intimate partner, or best friend) make up the inner circles, while acquaintances and strangers take up space in the outer circles (see figure 1).

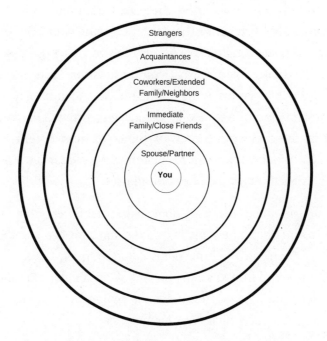

Figure 1. Risk Level in Relationships

Why is it often scarier to express our feelings, thoughts, needs, and wants to those closest to us? It is because there is a greater risk involved; we have more at stake, and therefore more to lose, with our loved ones. Because we are wired for connection with others and need relationships for our very survival, real or perceived threats to our relationships activate our fight, flight, or freeze response, making it extremely difficult to communicate clearly and assertively. The challenge is greater with those closest to us, but it's ultimately more important—and more rewarding!—to express ourselves authentically, including our differences, to those with whom we have important relationships.

Sometimes self-awareness and clear communication skills aren't enough to prevent others from crossing your boundaries. In certain situations, you will be required to take assertive *action* to reinforce your verbal communication. You may need to leave a conversation, hang up the phone, break off a relationship, stop responding to texts, take away your teen's car keys, or stand in the doorway to prevent someone from entering your home. Consider the woman in the following scenario who stood by her word and enforced her boundaries:

*I brought a newborn baby home with strict orders from the doctor to have no visiting kids in the home for two months. My sister wanted to bring her children over, but I was assertive and firm in saying no. She showed up one evening with her kids, hoping that I'd make an exception and let her family in to meet their baby cousin. I stood at the door and reiterated the doctor's orders. I feel bad that she became upset, but I don't regret standing my ground. I'm proud of myself and know it was the right thing for me to do.*

This courageous new mom *literally* took a stand to back up her words: she stood in the doorway and didn't let her relatives in! Saying the words is often easier than actually backing it up. Interestingly, the above example also highlights a recurring pattern I've noticed in my clinical practice—women are often willing to be assertive on behalf of someone else! In this case, allowing her sister and children to come over would have potentially put her baby at risk. I wonder if she would have been as firm if she were under doctor's orders not to have visitors for the sake of her *own* health. Have you noticed this pattern in your own life? Think about how it feels to stand up for yourself compared to asserting yourself on another's behalf.

When you are able to *express yourself* clearly and consistently, it will lead to stronger *connections* with others.

## Self-Expansion

Part of healthy assertiveness is the ability to speak up and stand up without silencing or disregarding someone else or violating his or her rights. Too often, differences between people result in a power struggle of whose opinion or feelings or ideas are "right" or "better." It absolutely does not have to be this way! An assertive woman can "hold space" in a conversation—and in her mind and heart–for another person's unique perspective or experience. In this way, we can expand our own awareness to include understanding and empathy for others.

Holding space for another person to have a different response or opinion than the one you express is not the same as agreeing with him or her or "giving in." It is developing the ability to allow for another person's feelings, thoughts, needs, or wants to be *different* than your own and yet still valid and valued. To illustrate, here's a simple conversation I've had dozens of times with my children about doing their home responsibilities:

> *"Have you completed your daily jobs yet?"*

> *"Not yet, Mom. I really don't want to take out the trash today or clean my room. I'm sooooo tired. Can I just watch TV for a while?"*

> *"So, you're really tired, you've had a long day at school, and you'd rather watch TV right now and not do your jobs. I hear you, son…AND you still need to finish your jobs before you watch TV. Turn it off right now or you will not be able to watch TV even after your jobs are done."*

In this conversation, I tried to hold space for my son to have and express different thoughts, feelings, wants, and needs in the conversation while simultaneously asserting myself and

25

holding him accountable for his responsibilities. This conversation could have easily turned into a power struggle whereby I defended how right I was about the fact that he needs to get his work done first (which has also happened many times, too). Or I could have complained about how often we have this same conversation. Or I could discount what he was expressing by saying something like, "You think you're tired? I've been going nonstop since early this morning, and I don't get a recess. You don't know anything about being tired!" But I'm grateful that I had the insight to hear him out (that time) and validate a different view while still holding him to the expectation of completing his chores. *Self-expansion*, or openness to hearing another's experience, is the path to developing more *compassion* in your heart and in your actions.

In summary, assertiveness is *not* being rude or pushy; it's the ability to both recognize your relationship patterns and identify and manage your emotions so you can take a stand for yourself or others. Assertiveness also includes being willing to use congruent body language to back up your words with actions when words are not enough. Finally, it also means being open to listening to and validating another person's differing experience. Now that we're on the same page with our definition of assertiveness, the following chapter will explain the connections between attachment, emotions, and potential challenges you may face in becoming more assertive.

To summarize, here are the five skills of assertiveness and the benefits you will achieve as you develop each skill:

| Assertiveness Skills (5 S's) | Benefits (5 C's) |
| --- | --- |
| self-reflection | clarity |
| self-awareness | confidence |
| self-soothing | calmness |
| self-expression | connection |
| self-expansion | compassion |

# CHAPTER 2

# Attachment, Emotions, and Assertiveness

Now that we've identified what assertiveness is and explored a few scenarios that required assertiveness, let's look at the origin of when and how you first learned to express yourself in your family. While assertiveness is focused on speaking up in a specific situation, our overall ability and willingness to communicate is influenced to a large part by our *past* relationship experiences, particularly those with our early caregivers. This emotional bond with another person is called an *attachment*.

Our early attachment relationships provide a template for future relationships. Though of course not guaranteed to dictate behavior, this template guides how we see ourselves, how much we trust others, what strategies we use to manage our emotions, and how confident we are in sharing ourselves. Our attachment style influences our comfort level and skill level when it comes to being assertive.

Understanding your attachment style is crucial to developing assertiveness. Why? Because it has largely influenced your core beliefs about yourself and relationships. Your attachment style has also shaped your communication patterns: from your early relationships you learned what feelings, thoughts, needs, and wants were okay to acknowledge and express. Knowing how you developed your relationship patterns can empower you to make sense of why it may be difficult for you to speak up, make requests, and advocate for yourself.

Remember the case example of Ella from chapter 1 who didn't like having sex? Let's continue the story. As Ella understood more about the development of her relationship pattern and attachment style (avoidant, but we'll get to the different styles shortly), she was able to identify, name, and experience the vulnerable emotions—loneliness, sadness, and fear—she had detached from when she was young. Through this process, Ella developed empathy for her younger self as a scared child and as a scared newlywed who was ill prepared for sexuality and marriage. She took responsibility for *her* part of the distant relationship pattern in her marriage and was able to see the subtle and the not-so-subtle ways that she was rejecting Lonnie. Ella and I worked together to help her identify and communicate her feelings, thoughts, needs, and wants—first in the therapy office with me and then with her husband, Lonnie. As she felt stronger and more connected to herself, she was able to share with Lonnie how scared and alone she felt as a child and how she had learned to cope with conflict by avoiding emotions. Ella's marital progress owed a lot to the process of her identifying and understanding the relationship and emotion patterns she learned as a child and how they had been replayed in the marriage. Improvements were also an outcome of her developing the skills to share more of herself (her thoughts, feelings, needs, and wants) with Lonnie.

As Lonnie sensed the relationship shifting, he started going to individual therapy to help him deal with some anxiety that had surfaced as a result of Ella's personal growth. As their levels of self-awareness and emotional intimacy grew, their sex life improved (which they were both very happy about). While they continue to experience periods of tension and relationship disconnection, just like every couple, they are better equipped to deal with their differences in ways that foster emotional closeness instead of distance.

## Looking Through an Attachment Lens

I've mentioned attachment theory a few times in this book already, but here's where we are going to go into it in more detail. Why do you need to know this stuff? Because I think it's one of the most helpful theories I've learned both personally and professionally, and I believe that learning to view yourself and others through an attachment lens will be incredibly helpful to you. A basic understanding of attachments is a foundational element of the assertiveness skills in this book. Without it, learning to effectively assert yourself and lead a more fulfilling life becomes much more difficult. With this in mind, as you read through this chapter, I invite you to consider how attachment theory applies to your own experiences as a child.

First introduced by psychologist John Bowlby (1958), attachment theory suggests that humans have an innate physiological need to form an emotional bond with caregivers and that having a strong bond is crucial to healthy development. After observing the distress patterns of institutionalized infants separated from their parents, Bowlby and his colleague James Robertson noticed progressive and predictable patterns of behavior in these children after separation. First, children *protested*, visibly upset by the separation from their caregivers. Next they sunk into *despair*, becoming apathetic and withdrawn from others. Finally, after continued separation, the children became *detached* and nonresponsive.

Bowlby also identified four components of attachment that children naturally develop around to maintain connection with their caregiver:

1. Proximity maintenance: the desire to be near attachment figures, to maintain physical closeness.

2. Secure base: the role the caregiver or attachment figure plays, and from which the child can explore the larger world (have you ever seen a toddler walk away from her parent and then check back to make sure the parent is still there? This is a normal part of the attachment process).

3. Safe haven: the return to the caregiver for a kiss or hug (when that same toddler feels scared or threatened, she will return to the caregiver for comfort).

4. Separation distress: the emotional upset exhibited by young children when they are separated from their parent or caregiver (a common example of this is a toddler's emotional protest when she is left with a babysitter for the first time).

How have these concepts manifested in your childhood or adult life and in the lives of your children or other young children you know? This attachment behavior in children is thought to be part of the evolutionary process, hardwired into humans in order to ensure the survival of our offspring. As children are helpless for their first few years (while other mammals can walk and feed themselves within minutes of birth), this attachment style ensures that a caregiver will provide for the child's basic physical and emotional needs, thus increasing her chances of survival.

In our early attachment relationships, we formed a *relationship template* and developed our view of ourselves and our expectations of others. If your caregivers were loving and generally responsive, you likely developed a sense that you are lovable, that relationships are dependable, and that people are trustworthy. In other words, you are more likely to feel a general sense of worthiness and a sense of safety in *future* relationships. If your caregivers were unpredictable, you may have grown up wondering if you are worthy of love, and you may have a nagging sense of fear and worry about whether other people will really love you and be there for you. If your early relationships were often neglectful and/or rejecting of your emotions and needs, then you may have developed an invisible shell as a way to protect your unmet needs and invalidated emotions. You may have learned to survive by detaching from or denying your feelings and needs.

In a similar way, our attachment needs drive our intimate adult relationships (Hazan and Shaver 1987). Similar patterns of protesting, despairing, and then detaching can be seen when an adult's important relationships are threatened by illness, betrayal, fear of abandonment, and other factors. The general attachment style developed throughout earlier life can also be seen in adult relationships, particularly with intimate partners.

The four attachment components present in childhood—proximity maintenance, secure base, safe haven, and separation distress—are also seen in adults. If you've ever been "in love" you probably know that feeling of wanting to spend time with and be close to your beloved. This is similar to *proximity maintenance*. Have you ever felt inspired by being loved? Like you could achieve almost anything? This feeling is like an adult *secure base*: when you know you are cherished you feel more confident to try new things. There's nothing like coming home to a big hug after a difficult day or hearing before a big work presentation the encouraging words, "You can do this. I believe in you." These are examples of an adult version of *safe haven*. *Separation distress* can occur when adults are separated from loved ones. Think about the distress and tears that arise when you say good-bye to your partner as he or she leaves the country for a year to serve in the armed forces, or when your child is ill in the hospital for a long stretch and you have to leave him or her to care for other family members.

## Three Attachment Styles

Building on Bowlby's work on attachment theory, colleague Mary Ainsworth (1979) designed "The Strange Situation," a structured way to observe the attachment relationships between a caregiver and child at twelve months old. Ainsworth identified basic childhood attachment styles based on patterns of interaction observed by toddlers in a laboratory setting. After the toddlers were systematically separated and reunited with their mothers, three general attachment categories emerged:

*Secure* (60%): distress when separated from caregiver, joy upon reunification with caregiver, ability to be close to others, trusting of others to meet needs

*Anxious* (20%): distraught upon separation, difficult to soothe upon reunification, clingy and overwhelmed

*Avoidant* (20%): minimal distress upon separation, does not seek contact when the caregiver returns

Interestingly, the percentages of adults who fall into each of the three attachment styles are roughly the same percentages as the children categorized in Ainsworth's research.

My personal and clinical experience has demonstrated that these basic relationship styles—secure, anxious, and avoidant—continue into adolescence and adulthood. And not *only* in our love relationships. Wherever we go, we take our attachment styles with us: into the workplace, into friendships, community groups, family relationships, and more.

Because our particular way of relating and getting our emotional needs met is the only way we know, it's possible to not be aware that different attachment styles and patterns exist. It's easy to think that *everyone* does relationships like you do. It is usually when our way of being in relationships causes us pain that we start reflecting on our own attachment style and patterns. This process of reflecting on your own history and patterns can sometime elicit difficult emotions and memories. It's normal to feel some discomfort or hesitation. However, this knowledge will allow you to see yourself and your current relationship patterns more clearly. The first step in this self-reflection process is getting familiar with your basic attachment style. Let's explore this further.

## AWARENESS EXERCISE
# What's Your Adult Attachment Style?

Let's bring this attachment style closer to home for you. Read the following statements and decide which of the *types* best describes you.

**Type 1**

- I often rely on others' approval to feel good about myself.

- I worry about my loved ones when we are physically apart.

- I often worry that I'll unintentionally push people away.

- I usually want to be closer to my friends, family, and lover than they want to be to me.

**Type 2**

- I frequently feel suffocated in relationships, especially with intimate partners.

- I feel best about myself when I'm independent and autonomous.

- I have been labeled aloof or distant in more than a few different relationships.

- I often wonder why other people get so upset about trivial things.

- I tend to let things "roll off of my back."

### Type 3

- I like being with loved ones and also spending quiet time alone.

- I don't worry much about my loved ones when we're apart.

- I feel things deeply, but I rarely "lose my cool."

- Most of the time, I am aware of what I am feeling inside.

- I have rarely felt smothered or suffocated in my love relationships.

### Key:

1 = Anxious attachment style

2 = Avoidant attachment style

3 = Secure attachment style

Keep in mind that attachment styles aren't "good" or "bad"—they just *are*. Being aware of your style will help you understand why certain aspects of speaking up may be difficult for you. Understanding your style will also help you pinpoint specific aspects of connection and communication where you can learn and grow. Most important, these styles are not cast in stone. While they tend to be enduring, attachment styles are also flexible and can evolve. You can develop a more secure style through psychotherapy, doing the hard work of growing in your close relationships, and putting into practice the concepts and skills in this book. In fact, that is one of my hopes for you as you make your way through this book—that you will, over time, develop a more secure style and a higher level of differentiation. What's "differentiation," you ask? Read on to find out.

# Differentiation

Attachment theory is based on the assumption that we are emotionally interconnected with one another. This interconnectedness is a core assumption in family systems theory, which is the assertion that a family makes up a "multiperson unit" that has its own characteristics and qualities and operates as a whole. In the previous chapter, we talked about how humans are wired for connection and closeness with others, and how we are born with the desire and capability to form lasting relationships. However, equally important to our discussion of assertiveness is how, in addition to being interconnected, we are simultaneously individuals with unique feelings, thoughts, needs, and wants.

We are both unique individuals *and* closely connected to others. Our ability to navigate the tension between our desire for individuality and our desire for connection through relationships is called *differentiation*. "Differentiation is the ability to maintain your sense of self when you are emotionally and/or physically close to others—especially as they become important to you" (Schnarch 1997, 56). It also includes the ability to engage in life from a place of authenticity and integrity instead of from a "false self" or a "pretend self" that often develops to avoid conflict, keep the peace, or placate others. Finally, differentiation of self involves the ability to distinguish thoughts and feelings and to take action from a mature and thoughtful place, instead of responding from a place of emotional reactivity (Bowen 1976).

## Low-Level Differentiation

Families with a lower differentiation level will resist a family member's attempt to assert herself in ways that challenge family norms, break family rules, or threaten family identity. Considering the family as a single unit, it makes sense that the group would exert pressure on the person who is differentiating in order to reduce anxiety and to maintain the status quo, or homeostasis. Families with low levels of differentiation are often called *emotionally fused* or *enmeshed* because they have a hard time knowing whose feelings and thoughts belong to whom.

An example of a family with a lower level of differentiation is a family who highly values formal education and expects *all* family members to earn advanced degrees. This family will have a more difficult time supporting and celebrating a daughter's decision to go to cosmetology school to become a hair stylist.

Or consider a family wherein the father is addicted to prescription medication. All the children are aware of the problem, but the unspoken rule is to "just act as if nothing is wrong." If one day at dinner someone asks, "Why is it that we never talk about Dad's addiction?" the response is stunned looks on family members' faces while the anxiety level in the room rises. The oldest child might try to quickly shut down that conversation by changing the topic to a sporting event, or the mother might express anger at the child who broke the "rule" and blame her for always ruining family dinners.

These two concrete examples of low-level differentiation are very overt. However, most behavior that indicates differentiation is a lot subtler. Expression of a certain emotion or a seemingly insignificant decision that goes against the family norm can also be signs of differentiation of self. Think of a toddler throwing a tantrum in a crowded mall. That is a sign of differentiation! Her screeching or behavior is clearly saying, "I'm not at all happy that we have to leave right now! I want a cookie!"

A parent with a lower level of differentiation would likely become emotionally flooded in such a situation and have difficulty separating her child's emotions from her own. She may experience a sense of shame and become increasingly self-conscious that the people walking by are thinking that she is a "bad mom who can't control her kid." She might grab her child by the arm and drag her to the closest bench where she scolds her and squeezes her arm harder while in a whisper-yell (I'm sure you're familiar with a mother's whisper-yell because your mom used it, and you might too!) she insists that her daughter stop crying or she'll have to take away her favorite stuffed animal.

## High-Level Differentiation

Using the same tantrum scenario, a highly differentiated mother would likely remain calm, pick the child up, and walk to the car without hurting or yelling at her child. This mother might say to herself, "I pushed her too far past naptime. I don't blame her for having a meltdown. I probably should have headed home an hour ago." Not only is she able to use her thoughts to keep calm and make sense of the situation, she is able to respond to herself and her child with compassion. She may do what she can to soothe her daughter on the way to the car by singing her favorite lullaby.

Families with higher levels of differentiation are able to accept a broader range of behaviors and expressions of unique feelings, thoughts, needs, and wants without raising the anxiety level to intolerable levels that feel threatening and overwhelming. Family members are able to act from a thoughtful place.

Here's another example of a family who has moved to the higher end of the differentiation continuum: my family of origin. We were raised in Los Angeles in a devout and highly religious home; however, many of my siblings, now all well into adulthood, no longer affiliate with the religion of our childhood even though my parents are still active in the faith. Even though they are no longer a part of our "family's faith," they continue to be included and accepted by the larger family group and are supported in their life choices. We can accept when a family member exhibits or expresses *difference*. My youngest sister, Sarah, is an award-winning tattoo artist and is, herself, covered with tattoos…and a few piercings. Her appearance is *very* different from the rest of us, who have a more conservative look. Yet Sarah and her own little family are embraced, included, and loved wholeheartedly by the group.

## What Does Differentiation Have to Do with Assertiveness?

The ability to be assertive—to clearly and confidently express your feelings, thoughts, needs, and wants even when they differ greatly from others who are important to you—is essentially an expression of *differentiation*. Assertiveness is a way that you express *difference* while remaining *connected*. Whether it's with family, colleagues, neighbors, or acquaintances, you can use the tools in this book to assert yourself—to express difference.

Here is a visual illustration of differentiation (see fig. 2): On the lower-level end of the differentiation continuum, you'll notice that "self" and "others" almost completely overlap. This represents emotional fusion or enmeshment—it's not clear whose thoughts, feelings, needs, and wants are whose. On the higher-level end of the continuum, "self" and "other" have a lot less overlap and yet are still connected.

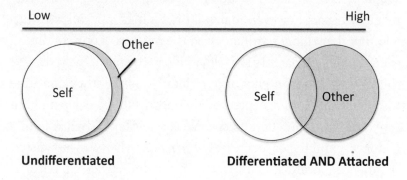

Figure 2. Differentiation Continuum

Now that you have the basics down, let's explore a bit more about your family of origin's level of differentiation and bring it close to home, literally.

AWARENESS EXERCISE
# Exploring Family Differentiation Level

Consider the following questions regarding your level of differentiation in your family of origin:

- Were certain emotions unacceptable to express in your family?

- How did your family respond when you voiced small differences of opinion (for example, wanting to go to a different restaurant or to watch a different TV show)?

- Think about your family identity or how you define yourself as a family unit. Complete this sentence: Our family is _____ (athletic, musical, funny, educated, hard workers, alcoholic, troubled, etc.).

- How did your family respond when someone varied from or challenged this family identity? Was difference tolerated but accompanied by high anxiety (medium level), punished (low level), or accepted or even celebrated (high level)?

- Based on your answers above, would you place your family of origin on the lower or the higher end of the differentiation continuum?

- On a scale from 0 (lowest level) to 10 (highest level), what differentiation score would you give your family of origin?

## AWARENESS EXERCISE
# Exploring Current Differentiation Level

Consider the following questions regarding your current comfort level in one of your closest adult relationships (lover, partner, best friend, closest family member):

- Are there certain emotions that you can't share with this person?

- How does he or she respond when you express a small difference of opinion (for example, how to spend the weekend or how to celebrate a special occasion)?

- Think about your own identity or how you describe yourself. Complete this sentence with three adjectives: I am _____.

- Do you show all of these characteristics when you are with your loved one?

- Would you describe yourself differently when you're with acquaintances?

- Based on your answers above, would you place yourself on the lower or the higher end of the differentiation level?

- On a scale from 0 (lowest level) to 10 (highest level), what differentiation score would you give yourself?

# The Intersection of Attachment Style and Differentiation

Now that you've been introduced to three general attachment styles and to the concept of differentiation, let's look at how they intersect. Take a look at Figure 3. If you lean toward an *anxious* attachment style, you likely have a *lower* level of differentiation and *higher* need for closeness and connection. Anxious-style individuals tend to want to be closer than others want to be to them, and avoidant-style individuals are comfortable with more distance or separateness in relationships.

If you lean toward an *avoidant* style, you are more likely to have a *low* level of differentiation and a *lower* desire for a close emotional connection. See where the *secure* style is located? It's at a *high* level of differentiation and right in the *middle* when it comes to desire for separateness.

A person with a secure style can be comfortable being emotionally close and connected; she also doesn't fall apart when there is separation or distance. Ironically, the ability to stand on your own two feet and have a strong sense of who you are allows you to develop healthier relationships, to reach out for support, to express difference, and to offer support to and tolerate the differences of others.

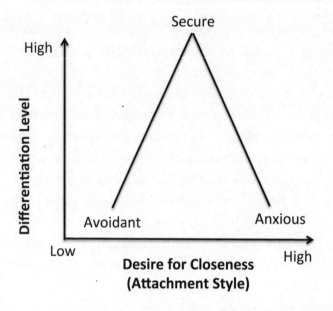

Figure 3. Attachment Style and Differentiation Level

If these concepts are new to you, you may feel slightly (or completely) overwhelmed by this new way of understanding relationships. Don't worry! Please continue reading on and considering these concepts. As you work your way through this book, these ideas will become clearer and more meaningful.

## Attachment, Differentiation, and Assertiveness

So how do attachment styles and levels of differentiation directly relate to assertiveness? Each attachment style has patterns of emotional management and relationship engagement that shape our ability and willingness to be assertive in a variety of human connections, whether romantic, familial, friendship, or work connections. And each emotional management pattern and relationship pattern has its own challenges.

The following is an overview of the attachment styles and their relational characteristics, differentiation level, emotional styles, and assertiveness challenges. (You can also download this overview in handy chart format at **http://www.newharbin ger.com/33377.**)

## Anxious Attachment Style

**Characteristics:** Clings to relationships; is anxious about being separate or being abandoned; is easily overwhelmed by emotions; has difficulty separating thoughts and feelings

**Differentiation Level:** Low

**Barriers to Assertiveness:** Is afraid to speak up for fear of creating distance or rejection; has fear of overwhelming the other person; lacks ability to identify emotions

**Assertiveness Approach:** Hesitant

**Assertiveness Goals:** Make sense of one's attachment style; identify feelings, thoughts, needs, and wants; develop emotional management strategies; build communication skills

A woman with an anxious attachment style may feel dependent on her relationships to feel good about herself. She may be viewed as clingy and also seen as somewhat "emotionally high-maintenance," as she often needs reassurance that she is loved. Women with an anxious attachment style are commonly overwhelmed with emotions (particularly worry) and fear of being abandoned or forgotten.

Individuals with an anxious attachment style face certain challenges when it comes to being assertive. These include a feeling that there are too many needs to be addressed, a fear of not being heard, feeling overwhelmed often, and difficulty sorting through emotions. When someone with an anxious style *does* decide to speak up, she often says too much and appears overly emotional to others. In order to address these challenges, individuals with this attachment style will strive to manage emotions, build communication skills, and develop a stronger sense of self and difference.

## Avoidant Attachment Style

**Characteristics:** Is uncomfortable being too emotionally close to others; feels content interacting on a surface level; is often unaware of thoughts and feelings

**Differentiation Level:** Low

**Barriers to Assertiveness:** Is often detached from emotions, especially during conflict or stress; has discomfort in discussing emotions for fear of getting "too close"; believes that it's better to just "let things go"

**Assertiveness Approach:** Guarded

**Assertiveness Goals:** Make sense of one's attachment style; acknowledge value of close relationships and interdependence; connect to emotions; identify feelings, thoughts, needs, and wants; and develop communication skills

Women with an avoidant attachment style tend to minimize or deny the need for close relationships and become uncomfortable when others become too close emotionally. They tend to be less aware of their emotions and minimize the importance of feelings. In their own eyes, they don't let their emotions get the best of them, as they see themselves as level-headed. Others may perceive women with this style as somewhat aloof or detached.

Some of the challenges to assertiveness for a woman who has an avoidant attachment style are difficulty acknowledging and identifying emotions, a reluctance to trust that others will be responsive if she speaks up, and the belief that it's better to simply "let things go" rather than to address feelings and needs. Some goals to overcome these challenges are to develop an increased awareness of emotions, promote connections with others, and accept attachment needs and interdependence with others.

## Secure Attachment Style

**Characteristics:** Can form relationships and also feels comfortable alone; is able to manage emotions; can separate thoughts and feelings

**Differentiation Level:** High

**Barriers to Assertiveness:** May have difficulty identifying and articulating emotions, or lack confidence to be assertive directly

**Assertiveness Approach:** Confident

**Assertiveness Goals:** Develop emotional vocabulary; identify feelings, thoughts, needs, and wants; practice emotional management skills; develop and solidify communication skills

Individuals with a secure attachment style can be emotionally close in relationships but can also be comfortable spending time alone. They are able to identify and experience a full range of emotions, as well as tolerate intense emotions of others without being overwhelmed by them. They also have the ability to speak up and communicate their needs and feelings.

Women with a securely attached style are quite competent at acting and speaking assertively. Still, some barriers to assertiveness for those with a secure attachment style may exist, such as a lack of vocabulary to adequately express their emotions, a lack of confidence in their assertiveness skills, or a fear of hurting others' feelings.

## Emotions and Assertiveness

Now let's talk about the connection between *emotions* (also referred to as *feelings* throughout this book) and assertiveness. I define emotions as felt bodily sensations that offer information, guidance, and cues about our experiences. Our feelings give us direction about what we *want* (and what we don't want) and what we *need* in order to improve our lives and the lives of those around us. In other words, your uncomfortable emotions are red flags signaling you to pay attention to a certain situation—to make requests, to set boundaries, to make changes, to assert yourself. "Feel-good" emotions instruct you to do more or get more of whatever it is that is associated with positive feelings. If you disconnect from your emotions, you will lose valuable guidance in your effort to be assertive.

### The Cost of Avoiding Emotions and Assertiveness

Some women will deny or ignore difficult emotions, and avoid communicating their feelings, thoughts, needs, and wants in an effort to protect themselves and their connections with others. However, if this describes you, know that this pattern can do great damage in the long run to both your well-being and your relationships. What happens when needs and feelings go unacknowledged for too long? Below is a list of common responses from women I've surveyed. Notice which ones resonate with you:

- Those emotions get trapped inside and fester.

- My blood pressure rises.

- I get stressed out.

- I get headaches.

- I tend to overeat.

- I withdraw and get depressed.

- I start worrying.

- I get really irritable.

- I feel on the verge of tears all the time.

- I take it out on my kids.

- After a while, I'll blow up at someone who doesn't deserve it.

There are many factors that contribute to our tendency to ignore emotional cues. As we've discussed, family patterns can play a big role in informing which emotions are "off limits." Information overload and constant stimulation of our senses through the media can be distracting and impede our ability to tune in to emotional cues. There are also other societal factors that have reinforced a general pattern of ignoring or silencing women's emotions that we'll go into in more detail in the following chapter.

For now, let's bring this concept to a more personal level. What emotions signal that you are not speaking up and sharing your feelings, thoughts, needs, and wants in your relationships? My big red flags are the feelings of resentment and exhaustion. We'll return to the idea of resentment later on in this book. But first, take a few minutes to explore your cues that you're emotionally disconnected or not being assertive.

## AWARENESS EXERCISE
## Cues That You're Not Being Assertive

What internal and external cues do you experience when you are not addressing your emotions and relationship issues in a direct and clear way? Consider physical bodily cues, thought patterns, and behavioral patterns.

## The Benefits of Cultivating Emotional Awareness

During the last few decades, compelling scientific evidence has emerged about the crucial role emotions play in all aspects of our lives. "Researchers have found that even more than IQ, your emotional awareness and abilities to handle feelings will determine your success and happiness in all walks of life, including family relationships" (Gottman and DeClaire 1992, 20). Though many women fear that sharing their feelings with others may hurt their relationships, emotional management and the ability to communicate are central to strengthening relationships in all areas of life. Researchers studying adult attachment suggest that the ability to share emotions in relationships, to allow yourself to be heard, and to hear and validate another's vulnerable emotions are key to developing intimacy and secure attachments.

Sharing your honest feelings in meaningful and powerful ways with others, in word and action, plays a large part in the development of healthy intimacy and connection with others. One memory aid that helps with this concept is to imagine that the word "intimacy" is pronounced "intomeesee," as in "into me, see"—as though a request: "Will you see into me?" The longing of every heart is to be seen and understood, to be cherished, to have emotional needs responded to in loving ways, and to be accepted—in other words, to be securely attached. The ability to share your honest emotions—both joy and pain—paves the way for deeper connections in all relationships. Developing skills to share what's in your heart with another person is one of the most important skills you can develop in life. Expressing more-vulnerable emotions (such as fear, longing, and sadness) in your relationships tends to draw others closer to you and can elicit more nurturing and gentle responses from the people who matter most.

## Feelings, Thoughts, Needs, Wants

In addition to sharing our feelings, assertiveness also includes being aware of and expressing our thoughts, our needs, and our wants to others. In our lived experience, feelings, thoughts, needs, and wants are interconnected and inform each other. We don't actually experience them as separate entities. In later chapters, we will explore ways to sort thoughts and feelings, but, for now, it's enough to say that *thoughts* are primarily in your head and *feelings* primarily reside in your heart (and the rest of your body).

Your feelings and your thoughts offer crucial information about what you need and what you want. But what is the *difference* between a need and a want? I distinguish needs from wants by deciding whether or not you can thrive physically, emotionally, and relationally without them. If you can't survive or thrive without them, they are needs. Wants are more in the category of "it would be nice if…" or "I'd really like it if…"

While these four things—feelings, thoughts, needs, and wants—are all connected, when you're trying to clearly communicate and assert yourself it's important to draw distinctions among them. This sorting process is a key part of self-awareness and self-reflection. Putting names to aspects of your experience helps you to feel "in charge" of it, to feel empowered, to take responsibility, and to take action. Here's an example to illustrate.

Thirty-five-year-old Irena came to therapy complaining of feeling overwhelmed and having no motivation; she was lethargic and didn't know why. There were no current significant stressors going on in her life. In fact, her situation had drastically improved in recent years. When she was a child, she experienced a chaotic home life, multiple moves due to evictions, financial instability, and taking on the role of caretaker of her two younger siblings. Now, as an adult, Irena's relationship with her partner, Joe, was going well. She sometimes felt burdened having to care for him with his chronic illness, but her current life was infinitely better than when she was younger. Irena couldn't understand why she wasn't ecstatic and energetic.

After a few therapy sessions, Irena began to realize that her exhaustion and lack of motivation was really a mixture of underlying anger and sadness related to unprocessed grief. Her mother died of cancer when Irena was only five. Here's an example of Irena sorting out and distinguishing her feelings, thoughts, needs, and wants during session 1 and again during session 4.

## Session 1

*Feelings:* Tired.

*Thoughts:* I shouldn't be tired. I have a great life.

*Needs:* I don't know what I need, and I don't know how I would know.

*Wants:* I want to be happy and have energy. I want to have a baby someday. I want Joe to be healthy.

## Session 4

*Feelings:* Mad and sad.

*Thoughts:* My parents left me to fend for myself and to take care of my siblings when I was still a kid. That is not right. That is not fair. I missed out on so much. My mom died and left me when I was five. At least my dad stuck around physically. His drinking made it so he couldn't really be there for me emotionally.

*Needs:* I need to be nurtured and taken care of, even now, as an adult. I need to figure out how to let Joe take care of *me.* I also need to practice self-care and self-compassion—to learn to nurture myself.

*Wants:* I want to experience more fun in my life. I want to learn how to paint and learn how to play tennis. I want to have energy and vibrancy.

Notice how by session 4 Irena was able to be a lot more specific in her descriptions. This is significant because the more she understands about her own experience, the more she will be able to share her feelings, thoughts, needs, and wants with her partner, friends, family, coworkers, and other important people in her life. This is the information Irena will need to access so she can assert herself, feel heard, and get her needs and wants met. (If you'd like to try the activity Irena did, download a worksheet for this from **http://www.newharbinger.com /33377.**)

In summary, our early childhood experiences shape who we are. They influence our attachment style, our differentiation level, our emotional awareness and management skills, and our ability to communicate assertively. Looking back and understanding your unique history can create an awareness that paves the way to true intimacy and closeness with others—and it can open up new possibilities for assertive communication. In addition to our earliest relationships, it's also important to consider barriers that are larger than individual and family patterns when talking about women, relationships, and communication.

CHAPTER 3

# Barriers to Assertive Communication

While attachment and differentiation apply to all sexes, let's explore what unique challenges women experience in speaking up and asserting thoughts, feelings, wants, and needs in a variety of situations. To get real-life examples, I surveyed numerous women and asked, "What keeps you from asserting yourself?" Some of their anonymous responses are listed below. As you read the following list, notice if any of these reasons sound familiar to you:

- I don't want to make the situation worse.

- I don't want others to think I'm controlling.

- I'm worried about how I will be perceived.

- I'm afraid the person won't like me anymore.

- I'm afraid I'll be misunderstood.

- I don't want to be shut out.

- I'm afraid of being fired from my job.

- I hate conflict and will avoid it at all costs.

- I want to be thought of as helpful, not selfish.

Looking at these responses, a very clear theme has emerged: women are concerned about damaging their connections and don't want to do anything that might threaten their relationships, rock the boat, or create conflict. This fits perfectly with attachment theory and what we know about our innate physical and psychological need for connection. Let's explore this idea further.

## Fear of Disconnection

Women's psychological research suggests that relationships are central to our lives and that, as we develop, we tend to frame our sense of worth by and derive meaning from how well we care for and are connected to those we love. This relational ethic is something that the world could use more of: less apathy, more connection, less indifference, more caring. However, this relational orientation has sometimes served to silence women's own voices.

The need to maintain connections with others exists no matter what your attachment style. Whenever connection with important people is threatened, we will do what it takes to try and maintain the connection. Many women will choose not to speak up. If you have an avoidant attachment style you likely remain detached when relationships are threatened because you learned that self-protection *will* maintain your relationships.

If you lean toward an anxious attachment style, you may be afraid that if you speak up you'll "lose control" of emotions and push others away. The theme is fear—fear of damaging the relationship and fear of disconnection. The desire to maintain close connections is not a weakness or flaw but a central need in *all* human beings. In fact, fostering close connections has historically been a strength of women. As we discuss throughout this book, emotional connection to others is a core need, not only essential to our emotional and psychological wellbeing but also to our physical survival. So it makes sense that we do whatever it takes to protect and preserve our relationships, even if it hurts us. Being socially isolated is a universal form of torture for human beings—think solitary confinement. (Although, I have to admit, that as a mother of four children and owner of a therapy clinic, temporary social isolations sound very appealing!)

Did you know that the pain of disconnection or social rejection triggers similar parts of the brain that are triggered by physical pain (Eisenberger 2015)? In some ways, social rejection can be *more* painful than physical pain because social pain can more easily be relived in our minds long after the specific situation has passed (Meyer, Williams, and Eisenberger 2015). It turns out that the childhood saying "Sticks and stones may break my bones but words will never hurt me" is not at all true. A more accurate saying might be "Sticks and stone may break my bones but words will hurt over and over again." I'll share a few personal examples to help illustrate.

When I was in sixth grade, another female student spread some lies about me to our other classmates, which resulted in the whole class turning against me. I sat alone at lunch and walked around by myself at recess. They threw things at me, stole things from my desk, called me names, and, after school, called me on the phone and harassed me with abusive words. While this bullying lasted for about a month, it felt like years. Even though this happened more than thirty-five years ago, as

I type these words I am noticing that my pulse is rising and I have a tightening sensation in my chest. I can recall the pain clearly—the pain of what it's like to be rejected.

Five years later, as an eleventh grader, I was walking with a group of fellow cheerleaders wearing bright blue and white uniforms in a crosswalk in front of our high school. It was Friday the thirteenth of September (I'm not even kidding), the first week of school, and the day of our very first football game of the season. As I walked and talked, I saw a flash of red out of the corner of my eye and felt myself flying like a rag doll through the air, then landing on the street. I was afraid to open my eyes because I didn't know what I'd find.

"What on earth happened?" I thought to myself. "Am I dead? Do I still have legs?" I soon learned that a woman driving a red car had hit three out of four cheerleaders in the crosswalk, and we were strewn across the street in front of North Hollywood High School. After an ambulance ride to the hospital and X-rays, I learned that I had broken my left leg and shoulder, damaged my knee, and that large areas of skin had been scraped off of my bare legs. As much as I try to recall and re-experience the physical pain of the injuries, I can't actually feel it. I actually giggle because it's such an unbelievable story!

The physical pain of being struck by a car and sustaining multiples injuries is lost to me, but the emotional pain of being a victim of bullying is something I won't ever forget. And so it really makes sense to me that emotional injury can be more painful and devastating than physical injury. Our physical bodies have built-in mechanisms for self-healing; however, sometimes we still require surgery, medication, or other interventions. We have a built-in system to help resolve emotional hurt, too; it's called attachment! We are designed to heal through healthy relationships. However, just like physical pain, resolving our emotional hurt may require a more conscious effort to heal. That's usually why people come in to see a therapist: they are feeling something painful, and no matter how hard they try they haven't been able to feel better.

We've all felt physical pain *and* the pain of being left out or rejected in some form or another, and we all learn strategies to protect ourselves from experiencing further pain. Rooted in our attachment styles, there are two basic ways that we try to preserve our relationships and protect ourselves from the pain of disconnection: by caring more or by caring less.

If you have an anxious style, you may tend to "care more" by wanting to be closer to others (perhaps more than they want to be close to you) and by becoming worried by separation and space. If you lean more toward an avoidant style, you may move more easily toward "caring less" as a strategy. You may be the one who is more likely to seek out or be more comfortable with emotional distance than others. We all use both strategies at different times throughout our lives to cope. But I'm willing to bet that you have a long-standing pattern of using one attachment style more than the other. Keep the dominant style in mind as you read on.

In an attempt to preserve an important relationship, you may hide or withhold parts of yourself that you fear might not be accepted by the other person; you don't want to create distance with your baggage or emotional idiosyncrasies. However, this very act of withholding can paradoxically hurt the relationship, as the person doesn't get to know the real you. So the fear of threatening a relationship is a very legitimate concern and is one that this book acknowledges and takes into account.

I'd like to now take a look at the broader, historical context for why women, as a group, may have a difficult experience with assertiveness.

# Cultural and Social Factors

In Western society, we tend to talk about issues and problems on an individual level, but individual and family relationship patterns are shaped and informed in large part by cultural norms in the larger society. When it comes to women, this is a particularly significant part of the discussion. Referring back to the surveyed responses of common reasons women don't assert themselves, notice that not one of them even gave a nod to family or cultural influences. I believe this speaks to the tendency in Western culture to idealize independence and self-sufficiency, and emphasize personal responsibility. Don't get me wrong here—I think these are generally good things! However, our culture's worship of individualism and independence neglects the interconnectedness of the individual with the culture in which she resides. The society in which an individual lives impacts every aspect of life, whether we are aware of it or not.

This tendency to attribute all of the power and responsibility to the individual—to ourselves—for our own pain can perpetuate feelings of hopelessness and isolation, and the belief that we should be able to solve our own problems. The tension between individualism and society is similar to our discussion in the previous chapter about the drive to be both a unique individual and part of a larger family system.

I've seen this play out in my own life many times. I recall a time about eight years ago when I felt overwhelmed at home, at work, and pretty much everywhere! My therapy practice had grown significantly, and I had several new employees. I was filling multiple roles as owner, therapist, and office manager. At home, my husband and I had recently had our fourth child. It was an exciting time with so many positive signs of growth on every front. The problem was that I was exhausted and struggling to keep up! I automatically attributed (perceived) shortcomings to individual flaws and personal deficits: *I'm not organized enough. I'm not taking good care of my health. I've got to plan better. I'm lazy.* As I reflected on my life and what needed to change, it dawned on me that there were a lot of gender-related cultural messages being played out in my thoughts, feelings, and behaviors that were preventing me from identifying what I wanted and needed.

It occurred to me to explore the question, "What would I do in this situation if I were a man?" The answer immediately came to my mind. I said to myself, "If I were a man, I would hire assistants, without guilt, and I would feel so good about myself and my successes." So that's what I did. I hired an office manager at work, we hired a home assistant at home, and I've never looked back. Societal messages are powerful and often underacknowledged in our individual-focused society. Therefore, I really want to devote some time to touching on some societal factors that have impacted our ability to assert ourselves.

Carol Gilligan (1982), a pioneer in women's psychological research, suggests that women tend to define and evaluate themselves based on their ability to care for others. This "ethic of caring" psychologically orients women toward maintenance of relationships and interpersonal connections. And if our very identity is defined in large part by our success in caring for and staying connected to others, then it makes sense that we would work hard to preserve our relationships—it is a way of protecting ourselves. Additionally, from a larger societal perspective, girls have generally been socialized to nurture, support, and care for others. As a result, girls may be more willing to put others' feelings and needs ahead of their own.

Consistent with Gilligan's theory, Dr. Jean Baker Miller and her associates of the Stone Center at Wellesley believe that human beings grow in and through relationships with others, and that relationships are shaped by societal factors. Miller's work, also called Relational-Cultural Theory, challenged and continues to challenge the prevailing belief that independence and autonomy, generally associated with masculine values, are the pinnacle of mental health. Due to societal expectations, Miller explains that "[w]omen have been so encouraged to concentrate on the emotions and reactions of others that they have been diverted from examining and expressing their own emotions…[They have] not yet fully applied this highly developed faculty to exploring and knowing themselves" (1987, 39).

This idea of a relational orientation is something that I personally value very highly, and yet, it can become a barrier to asserting my feelings, wants, and needs if I think there is any threat of damage to the relationship (I don't want to disappoint others or hurt anyone's feelings). The "ethic of caring" is certainly a double-edged sword; thinking and acting compassionately toward others is wonderful but can be problematic if taken to such a level that one's own needs are denied or neglected.

Cultural expectations and socialization processes often differ based on gender. We can see examples of this in the contrasting ways that men and women relate to and express assertiveness and their own emotional awareness. Beginning at birth, girls are generally given toys like dolls and kitchen sets—objects that encourage nurturing and caretaking—while boys are generally given toys like balls and trucks, which invite more physical activity, autonomy, and competitiveness (Coltrane and Adams 2008). Parents tend to be more controlling of girls' behavior than they are of boys' behavior, and to encourage girls more often to behave cooperatively and prosocially. Family chores are often assigned along traditional gender lines, with girls given chores centered around housework and childcare, while boys are given responsibilities outside of the home, like taking out the trash and doing yard maintenance (Etaugh and Bridges 2015).

Fortunately, during the past several decades girls have been more encouraged to pursue competitive sports, academic achievement, and leadership opportunities, allowing them to develop a broader range of skills and capabilities, and to integrate connection to others with a sense of autonomy and strength (Coltrane and Adams 2008). This shift opens up new possibilities for both strong relationship bonds and higher levels of self-development.

## Ladder and Field Models

Another societal barrier that creates difficulty for women to be authentic and assertive in relationships is the cultural norm of measuring our self-worth based on where we stand, or rank, *in comparison* to others. The question of who's stronger, who's smarter, who's right, who's thinner, and so forth sets us on the metaphorical rung of a ladder either above or below others. Metahistorian and social scientist Riane Eisler (1987) calls this a *dominator* model, led by hierarchies of domination through fear and force. Dominator cultures highly value characteristics and behaviors associated with masculinity and devalue those things connected with femininity and caretaking; they also have a high degree of institutionalized violence. This cultural pattern spills into our personal and work relationships through the assumption that we are always in competition with others— and that we must rank above them in order to be valued.

I like to use the analogy of a ladder to represent this pattern of ranking. Imagine all of us as rungs of a ladder. In order to be successful, you have to step on someone else and push them down to move yourself upward. This is so ingrained in our interactions that we may tend to interpret assertiveness in

65

others as threatening to our position on the ladder, inciting a defensive response. This may create an environment where the strongest and toughest person can climb up the ladder and access power over others who are weaker. Because of the comparative ranking in our society, assertiveness may be interpreted as aggression and a quest for power *over* others.

At its core, ranking and competing is about worth and connection. In a dominator model, worth is derived from social status, or how high you can climb on the ladder. An individual's worth is contingent on where she is in comparison to others. In this way of organizing ourselves, our worth is always being threatened because there will always be someone on rungs above us. At any time, we might be crawled over and pushed down, which, in a ranking system, means *worth less*.

On the other side of the spectrum from the dominator model is what Eisler calls a *partnership model*, organized by linking and connecting (instead of hierarchical ranking) and caring for others. This is similar to Gilligan's psychological concept of "ethics of care," and Miller's theory that we grow *toward, in,* and *through* healthy connections with others. Partnership societies are led by what Eisler calls *hierarchies of actualization*—individuals and organizations in positions of influence that aim to promote growth for *all* members. Instead of power *over* others, they have power to make a difference *for* others. Movement toward linking and connecting as a fundamental way of relating to others opens up opportunities for organizational and interpersonal communication that allows both parties to share vulnerable feelings and needs, and to be heard, understood, and valued. I call this the "field" perspective; there is no need to "one up" the other person or to put your feelings and needs above his or hers because the focus is on connecting not on competing, on linking not ranking. These are the very qualities that promote secure attachments, a climate of trust and respect, and healthy communication in all relationships; this perspective also allows for individuals to balance attachment and difference.

The ladder and field models also play out in smaller units of society, such as in the ways families or workplaces organize themselves and interact with each other. I have worked with couples who have internalized the belief that the male partner is "in charge," more capable, and has more important things to do and to say than the female partner (ladder model). Essentially, the man is superior to the woman and thus has power over her (fortunately, this paradigm seems to be changing). Another manifestation of the ladder framework I've observed is parents utilizing an authoritarian parenting style characterized by highly valuing conformity, rarely engaging in give-and-take dialogue, punishment for expressions of difference, and shaming. The parents maintain their rank through fear and force instead of love and connection.

Thankfully, there are families who employ a healthier style that are more akin to the field idea. Here's an autobiographical example excerpted from my journal:

*January 27, 2014*

*My husband was laid off from his job in Nov. and has been home full-time since then. I don't know how long this arrangement will last, but we have totally renegotiated our roles. Talk about flexible gender roles! He is now tracking children's scheduling and doing domestic chores (shopping, cooking, laundry, carpooling) while I put the pedal to the metal as the sole provider and PhD student. For the past week, we have officially and explicitly redefined our roles after a series of intense and emotional conversations. While we have always had role flexibility throughout our marriage, much of our basic stewardships fell generally along traditional gender expectations. This is the most "traditional" our roles have ever been, just in reverse gender expectations.*

*While my husband has done a lot of cooking throughout our marriage, and generally been in charge of Sunday dinners, he has also taken on the additional responsibility for gathering our family together. Since our oldest two children are not living at home, he is the one who reaches out to invite them for dinner or other family gatherings.*

*For the first time since having children—23 years—I've been able to let go of guilt or angst or tension about not "being there" to care for my children, or feeling like I "should" be with them even though I want to keep writing or working or creating. Our children are with their dad, so there is no reason for guilt! I had no idea the extent of the tension I have carried around in my muscles, my body—the tension between creativity and caretaking—until it had subsided. I have never felt so free and so relaxed and so nurtured. I have never felt like I really "should" want to be working or creating or writing or whatever. But now I am "supposed" to work. My family needs me in order to survive, to pay the bills, to continue our lives.*

*Oh, how those gender expectations run so deep…* (Hanks 2015, 64)

Now it's time for you to reflect on how your childhood family was and current family is fundamentally organized.

## AWARENESS EXERCISE
### Ladder and Field

Take a minute and think about how your early family relationships were (or still are) structured. Was your relationship with your parent(s) or caregiver(s) organized toward the ladder (competitive, power *over*) or the field end of the continuum (connecting, actualizing, power *to*)?

Think about your current home or employment situations. Is the organization based primarily on ranking or connecting?

# False Dichotomy: From Either/Or to Both/And

A larger cultural tendency is to view concepts and people in dualistic terms, as *either/or*. This perspective unnecessarily complicates relationships and communication. Because women are often oriented toward preserving relationships, this dualism is typically translated into a forced choice of self *or* other, win *or* lose, right *or* wrong. If forced to choose, many women put others' needs or happiness before theirs. This is primarily due to having little awareness or exploration of the paradigm allowing *both/and* or a middle ground.

Can you think of a time when you allowed others' preferences, needs, or feelings to take precedence over your own? If you are a parent, it likely happens every day! While this isn't a bad thing, it can become problematic if your feelings, thoughts, needs, and wants *always* get pushed aside in order to meet the needs of others. The good news is that you can challenge this false framework. Let me introduce you to one of the most important words I've ever known: and. Once you embrace the "both/and" in your relationships, new possibilities open up immediately.

For example, say you're in a heated conversation with your boyfriend because he came home late from work and didn't call you. You had planned to go out to dinner, and you were upset that you'd been waiting for him for an hour. The conversation quickly escalates. He starts bringing up how many times you've done the same thing to him so you shouldn't be mad. You accuse him of not caring about you. The intensity is rising. What both of you want is to be heard and validated, yet in the either/or paradigm, someone has to be *right* (and someone has to be wrong). It's human nature to want our view to be the correct perspective, the legitimate story, and so we work harder and harder to prove that we are right and the other person is wrong. This is where "both/and" can save both of you from escalating into a destructive power struggle. *Both* of you can have thoughts and feelings *and* they can be different *and* still valid.

In a both/and conversation with your boyfriend, you might say, "I am upset that you didn't call to let me know you'd be late. I've been waiting for an hour to go to dinner and I'm really hungry. I'm also scared that maybe I'm not important to you. Will you call me next time? I was worried about you. What was going on from your perspective?" You don't make him bad or wrong. You are simply expressing the impact of his behavior on you by sharing your thoughts and feelings. This approach will make it much less likely that he will immediately go into defense mode.

In a both/and conversation, he would be able to hear and validate your pain about his behavior by saying something like, "I can see that you're upset. I'm so sorry that I didn't call to let you know I'd be late and that you've been waiting for me—and feeling worried. I will really make an effort to give you a quick call or text next time. I was in an intense discussion with my manager about some problems we're having, and I wasn't watching the time. I apologize."

"And" creates space for you to be open-hearted to another person's complaints because you don't have to decide who is right or wrong, or whether he or she is the problem or you're the problem. There is room for the other person's perspective *and* your perspective, his or her contribution to the problem *and* yours. Both/and allows for emotional connection in relationships amid differing emotions, views, and opinions.

For a worksheet to guide you through conducting a both/and conversation, visit **http://www.newharbinger.com/33377**.

# Barriers to Assertiveness Can Be Overcome

As you can tell, there are many factors (both internal and external) that may impede your willingness and motivation to be assertive, perhaps the most fundamental being the fear of threatening a significant relationship. However, I challenge you to consider the cultural messages that impact your individual fears and perceived limitations. This will help you hold a larger context in mind as you learn how to assert yourself.

If you have feelings, thoughts, needs, and wants that go too long unknown or unmet, what could you lose? If you have these same things known and attended to, what could you gain? In later chapters, we will discuss how a willingness to share vulnerable feelings in relationships is the path to true intimacy with others. It's also the key to finding lasting satisfaction and contentment in your own life. As you move from an either/or mentality to both/and—and transition from a ladder framework that breeds the need to compare, out-do, and be right to a field framework that places you and others on equal ground—practicing assertiveness skills becomes easier.

In the following chapter, we will look more closely at relationship patterns, emotional coping styles, and messages about gender roles in your own family and their impact on your current attachment style and assertiveness struggles.

# CHAPTER 4

# Self-Reflection: Exploring Your Relationship Patterns

One of the most important factors that impacts your willingness to assert yourself as an adult is the general *attachment style*, or basic relationship template, you learned as a child. Your relationship template began forming during interactions with your earliest caregivers. Through your early, preverbal interactions, you gleaned whether you could trust that others would respond to or ignore your distress signals. You learned whether the world was safe or scary. You learned core messages about who you were in the eyes of and through the responses of your parents and caregivers.

This is not to say your attachment style develops solely on your caregiving relationships. Like most aspects of human development, your attachment style is influenced by a number of factors. Your basic temperament, your unique physiology, your gender socialization, your interactions with extended family members, your specific cultural expectations, and societal factors—such as availability of housing, food, and financial resources—all play a role in how you connect with others. Even if you're born into a nurturing and emotionally safe, stable family, outside events like war, death, trauma, and other stressors can also shape your attachment style, emotional patterns, and your experiences. Still, your earliest experiences with others profoundly impacted your attachment pattern.

Also rooted in your emotional patterns is your *level of differentiation* (discussed in chapter 2), that is, how you define and express your unique self within your family system. In addition to your attachment style, your differentiation level impacts your awareness and willingness to speak up and advocate for yourself and others. It also affects the level of expressed difference in thoughts and feelings you are afforded within the family system.

Here's an example of how early relationships impact attachment style and level of differentiation: Katie's father was a stern man who had little tolerance for her normal childhood playfulness and exuberance. As a toddler and young child, Katie's enthusiasm was met with austere, disapproving glances from her father and harsh shushes from her mother. Katie's expressions of excitement about what happened at school were curtailed by both parents in order to protect Dad from heightened anxiety that often led to angry outbursts and harsh punishments. In time, Katie learned to mirror her father's somber nature and to essentially cut off the passionate part of her natural expressiveness. Her parents didn't tolerate her differences, and so she muted her emotions and ideas for the sake of reducing anxiety for the family.

Can you guess what attachment style and level of differentiation Katie developed during the course of her formative years? She came to have an *avoidant* attachment style and a low level of differentiation, and she carried those patterns into adulthood.

When we talk about differentiation levels in this chapter, we'll be using a continuum from 0 to 10.

A rating of 0 means that your feelings run the show, you can't distinguish thoughts and feelings, you're emotionally reactive or overly compliant, or have little sense of which thoughts and feelings are yours and which belong to others. You have an extreme anxious or avoidant attachment style.

At the other end of the differentiation continuum is a 10. This represents an ability to distinguish thoughts and feelings clearly, express them directly, and act independently, in spite of pressure to conform. You have a strong sense of individuality and are able to maintain strong and healthy relationships. You have a secure attachment style.

# Connecting the Past with Present

Since I'll be asking you to dive deeper into your life experiences, it's only fair that I share more about my own history and development. Here's a peek into how my upbringing has impacted my general attachment style, my level of differentiation, and my willingness and ability to assert myself.

## My Early Attachment History

As the second oldest of nine children (yes, *nine*), I learned fairly early on how to take care of others. There was not a lot of individual one-on-one time with either of my parents, and I learned how to minimize my own feelings, thoughts, and needs for the sake of the family.

My mother, while wholeheartedly dedicated to caring for her family, was often on the brink of exhaustion trying to meet the needs of so many children. And who could blame her? My father, while equally dedicated to his family, worked hard as a musician and composer to provide a living for his ever-growing family. It seemed that the one who screamed and cried the loudest, or the child who was the youngest, got the immediate attention...and that person was generally *not* me. Instead, I would often be the one who jumped in to help.

So, I became fairly independent, compliant, and helpful; over time, I developed perfectionistic and people-pleasing tendencies, trying to win approval through being "good" and caring for others. On the outside, I was the epitome of a good girl, but inside I often felt disconnected, sad, and alone (which is ironic since I was surrounded by eight siblings). I was still a happy child, and had a lot of friends and a lot of fun, but there was a part inside that felt hollow. While I knew my parents loved and cared for me, I came to believe that their approval was contingent on my good, compliant behavior.

Shame and vulnerability researcher Brené Brown (2012) calls this "hustling for worthiness"—the belief that you have to *earn* love and belonging. This pattern of caretaking and pleasing contributed to the development over time of a *false self*, or a mismatch between my inner life and outer behavior; an anxious attachment style; and a fairly low level of differentiation. It was only after being a client in therapy starting in adolescence, and in learning about psychological theories, that I could make sense of the basic patterns I learned in childhood. Through identifying my attachment style, my family patterns, messages about emotions, and gender-related cues, I have come to better understand myself (including my general reluctance to act assertively) and to heal, gain insight, and develop a more secure attachment style.

Having a clear understanding of your attachment style and family patterns can help you empathize with yourself, heal any leftover or unresolved pain, and pinpoint areas you want to work on and skills you can develop.

To illustrate how to organize and make sense of your family relationships, you'll want to put together a basic relationship template based on what you learned in childhood. Let's look at mine as an example:

## My Family Relationship Template

Family relationship patterns: *I learned to get approval and attention by being good and compliant, looking good, taking care of my siblings, and being helpful and happy. I sensed that my parents were overwhelmed at times, so I learned to not be "needy." I learned how to speak and translate my dad's rooted-in-thought communication style and my mom's emotion-filled one.*

Family identity: *We are talented, bright, interesting, musical, spiritual, and special. My father and his side of the family are all entertainers, as were many of our neighbors and church community members.*

Emotional rules: *Don't be mad. Mad is bad. When I would protest, my parents used to say, "Don't cry or I'll give you a reason to cry!" which was threat of physical punishment. Smile, be nice, and it'll all work out.*

Gender roles: *From observing my parents' marriage, I learned that men are in charge, have autonomy inside and outside of the home, are smarter and more interesting, and are emotionally inaccessible. I learned that women are to sacrifice themselves and take care of others; appearance is very important, supporting the husband is key, and women's emotions are intense and overwhelming.*

Attachment style: *Anxious. In general, I experienced more anxiety and overwhelming emotions than detachment from my emotions. I recall being a preschooler and realizing that my parents were going to die at some point, and I wasn't sure who would take care of me.*

Differentiation level: *4*

Assertiveness approach: *Hesitant. Don't show "negative" emotions like mad or furious. Don't express strong opinions. I felt intense emotions but didn't know how to articulate and manage them.*

## Exploring Your Early Attachment History

Identifying your first memories can give you clues about your attachment style. If you determined in chapter 2 that you were generally anxious in your adult attachments, it is likely that your attachment style will have its roots in your earliest interactions. The same goes for secure or avoidant styles. The following questions will give you a sense of the patterns you learned in your infancy and childhood, and help you understand the relationship strengths and difficulties you now face.

### AWARENESS EXERCISE
### Early Attachment History

Consider the following questions regarding your childhood attachment experiences:

- What are your earliest childhood memories?

- What stories are told about you as a young child?

- How would you describe your relationship with your father?

- How would you describe your relationship with your mother?

- Which five words best describe your mother?

- Which five words best describe your father?

- Think of a time in your childhood when you were hurt or sick. Who did you go to for comfort?

- When you were a child, were there any other adults who cared for you?

(adapted from George, Kaplan, and Main 1985)

Now, take the time to reflect on your answers a bit. What you're looking for in the exercise above are *patterns*. Here are some patterns to watch for to help you identify and understand your basic adult attachment style:

**Anxious style**

- Is preoccupied with events in the past
- Past patterns still play out in present family relationships
- Past and present are blurred

**Avoidant Style**

- Is dismissive of importance of early relationships
- Doesn't offer detail/can't remember much
- Overvalues her autonomy and undervalues emotional connection

**Secure Style**

- Has a balanced, integrated story about her life
- Has an evolving understanding of relationships and emotions
- Is able to reflect on her own and others' behaviors and emotions

(Siegel 2010)

Here's more explanation about what your answers above indicate or what these questions are designed to elicit:

## What are your earliest childhood memories?

We tend to remember things that are emotionally charged in some way. These tend to shape our sense of self. Listen for emotional themes and tones in your narrative. Are your earliest memories accompanied by connection or disconnection with family members? Are your memories primarily with one person? Who? What emotions tie these memories together?

### What stories are told about you as a young child?

This answer may give clues to the role you played in your family and how other family members viewed you. If there aren't family stories about you as a young child, you may want to find out more about what was going on in your family life when you were a child. How does the lack of stories about you as an individual inform your sense of self and your place in your family?

### Which five words best describe your mother?

These descriptors will give insight into your overall template for female relationships. Are they all negative? Are they all glowing? Or some mixture of positive and difficult characteristics? A combination of good and bad aspects means that you can acknowledge the existence of all aspects of your mother, not just good and not just bad. This balance would indicate a healthy relationship pattern with women. If, for example, you describe your mother as a drama queen, it is likely that you expect that kind of behavior from other women in in your adult life too. Or perhaps you expect women to behave in very restricted and proper ways because your mother modeled these behaviors.

### Which five words best describe your father?

These descriptors will give insight into your overall template for male relationships. Are they all negative? Are they all positive? Or is there some mixture of positive and difficult characteristics? A combination of good and bad aspects likely indicates a realistic view of men. If, for example, you describe your father as selfish and irresponsible, it is likely that you expect that from men in your adult life too. Or perhaps you expect men to be totally selfless and hyper-responsible because your father modeled these characteristics.

### How would you describe your relationship with your father?

Your response here indicates how you likely expect to engage with men in relationships. If, for instance, it is warm and respectful, then you'll likely expect other men to treat you the same way. If your father was absent and you never knew him, you may expect other men to abandon you, too.

### How would you describe your relationship with your mother?

Your response here indicates how you likely expect to engage with women in your life. If, for instance, you describe your relationship as "two peas in a pod" or "your BFF," that indicates a low level of differentiation. If you describe your mother as critical and controlling, you may find that your female coworker and friends rub you the same way.

### Think of a time in your childhood when you were hurt or sick. Who did you go to for comfort?

Your answer will help you understand the physical and emotional availability of your caregivers and their level of responsiveness to your needs. I've had clients answer anything from, "I stayed home by myself while my parents worked" to "My dad stayed by my bedside, brought me chicken soup, and anything else I asked for. I could tell that it hurt him that I was sick." The first answer suggests a lack of nurturing, while the second response suggests overinvolvement and too much closeness.

**When you were a child, were there any other adults who cared for you?**

Your answer will help you understand whether you felt a sense of stability when it comes to caregivers. If there were consistent caregivers in your life, it is more likely that you would develop a secure attachment style. If you had inconsistent caregivers—perhaps you were in ten different foster homes by the time you were eighteen—it would be likely that you developed an insecure style (either anxious or avoidant).

# Integration

The hallmark of a securely attached style and a higher level of differentiation is *integration*: of good *and* bad in relationships and in people, in connection *and* separation, in thoughts *and* feelings. The goal of looking at your past history is to integrate it into your life's story. Even people who have experienced trauma and neglect can create a cohesive narrative or story about their life that makes sense. This integration in your mind (and in your body) is the hallmark of health.

In his groundbreaking book *Mindsight*, interpersonal neurobiologist Dr. Dan Siegel (2010) talks about two different types of memory: explicit and implicit. *Explicit memory* is memory that we recall as memory, while *implicit memory* is an experience that we are not aware of but that greatly influences our mental models and our priming, or what to expect in certain situations. Siegel uses the analogy of riding a bike to describe the difference between the two. When you hop on a bike and are able to ride it down the street, you are accessing implicit memory. When someone asks you about the first time you rode a bike, you draw upon explicit memory. The patterns, models, and expectations we carry with us are implicit—we aren't aware of their existence and yet they shape our lives in significant ways.

If somewhere in your history your caregivers were absent, inconsistent, or had unpredictable patterns of emotional responsiveness, you may naturally have some anxiety about how you emotionally attach to others. You likely developed an anxious style and a low level of differentiation. If you generally experienced responsiveness, attunement, and validation for your expression of thoughts and feelings that differed from your caregivers and other family members, you likely developed a secure attachment style. If your caregivers were emotionally detached, harsh, unresponsive, or neglectful to your emotional cues, then you are likely to have developed an avoidant/insecure style. It's important to remember that while you may experience characteristics of all the three categories of attachment, it's the predominant one that most informs your general attachment style. And…it can evolve!

## Attachment Wounds

Since all of us are raised by flawed humans (or wolves…just kidding), there will be gaps in our emotional and relational development. This is normal—life has its ups and downs, and children are exposed to how their caregivers handle unexpected or tough situations. However, if we have needs that are chronically neglected, unhealthy patterns that continue on, or experience situations or events that are traumatic (death or loss of a parent or family member, sexual or physical abuse, abandonment) these can create "attachment wounds," or particularly sensitive areas, in your adult relationships. Couples therapist and researcher Dr. Sue Johnson (2008) calls these wounds emotional "raw spots." She likens them to physical wounds we've all experienced—a bruise on your arm or even a hangnail that is painful to the touch—whereby you automatically pull back when someone goes to touch that area. The same thing happens with emotional boo-boos. We become hypersensitive and protective of these raw spots.

While attachment wounds are often talked of in the therapy world in terms of trauma, they aren't always due to a single event. Attachment wounds can be created by more subtle and pervasive hurtful relationship patterns that develop over time. Years of being verbally abused by your older sibling or rarely hearing that you are loved can create raw spots that continue on into your adult relationships.

One example of an individual who experienced difficulty in her emotional development (despite having a fairly functional family) was a client I once worked with. Gina was the third of five children born to loving parents. When Gina was a young child, her mother, the primary caregiver, suffered from deep depression, making it difficult to care for her children's physical needs, let alone be attuned to and responsive to their emotional needs. When she was only a toddler, Gina took the pain, sadness, and fatigue she saw in her mother's eyes as a reflection of her own lovability and worth. Not yet possessing the cognitive ability to make sense of the experience or self-differentiate, she absorbed her mother's emotions as a part of herself. This left Gina with a fear that she was somehow flawed or bad, along with a sense that she wasn't deserving of consistent nurturing.

This experience profoundly influenced Gina as she grew into adulthood. She kept her emotions and needs inside and didn't ask for what she wanted and needed. She also felt socially incompetent and believed that she wasn't as smart, attractive, or talented as her siblings. As an adult woman, Gina partnered with men who would treat her poorly. She had difficulty saying no to unwanted sexual advances and was taken advantage of.

This only reaffirmed her belief that she wasn't worthy of love and that she wasn't as good as the rest of her family.

I use this illustration *not* to place blame or fault on Gina's mother; too often, moms get scapegoated as the cause of their children's difficulties! Rather, I use this example to show how individuals from loving, relatively stable families still have attachment wounds to work through. Gina was not chronically abused as a child. She did not have a significant loss. Her story illustrates that *all* of us, even those from caring, dedicated families, have wounds or developmental gaps rooted in our early childhood experiences.

## Emotional Rules

Just as I learned as a child that certain emotions were off-limits, that I shouldn't express or even feel them, you likely drew some conclusions about what were and were not acceptable emotions based on your early experiences. Maybe some of these deep-seated beliefs have followed you into adulthood, or perhaps you've challenged them and sought a different emotional approach to life. Either way, it can be beneficial to explore the messages you learned concerning emotions.

To start, it's helpful to understand the six basic human emotions. These can give us a good starting point for understanding our internal human experiences. They are: happiness, sadness, surprise, fear, disgust, and anger.

In the coming chapters, you will learn more about expanding your emotional vocabulary and awareness, as well as tools and techniques to help you manage your emotions. For the purposes of this chapter, however, let's briefly look at the emotional environment of your childhood. Patterns of emotional expression, avoidance, and management create your emotional template and inform how you manage your emotions today.

Take a moment to recall your own emotions as well as those you witnessed from other family members. You might begin by asking yourself the following questions (available in worksheet format at **http://www.newharbinger.com/33377**):

- Which emotions were okay and which were not okay? Which emotions were given names and responded to?

- How often did your family members express vulnerable emotions (like sadness, fear, or loneliness)? How were these kinds of emotions responded to? In what ways?

- Which emotions did your parents have a hard time acknowledging or expressing?

- Did you experience any physical symptoms that had no obvious physical cause? Do you think they could have been a physical impact of suppressing emotions?

- What behaviors did you see your parents engage in when they were trying *not* to feel something?

Even if your early family life wasn't the most ideal, emotionally available environment, you can develop healthier ways to express emotions in relationships. Like most of the ideas in this book, identifying and managing feelings in a healthy way is a process of growth through practice!

# Gender Messages

Our gender and the messages we receive about gender in our families and in society play a significant role in identity development, informing not only who we are but what is expected of us. In every society and every family, gender carries certain implications, expectations, and meaning. We covered many of these messages in chapter 3 in the discussion on barriers to assertive communication.

The messages regarding what it means to be a female or male—what your options are for appropriate emotions, behaviors, goals, careers, talents, and capabilities—potentially begin at birth, or even *before* birth, when parents find out the sex of their child and begin different preparations for a boy or a girl. Gender affects every area of life, even when there really is very little difference between a male and a female child. You may recall from chapter 3 how the chores that are assigned to children and the amount of attention, control, or encouragement that a child receives are all based on how society—and family— views specific roles for girls and boys.

A primary influence on what you believe it means to be a girl or a woman is likely someone you had a close relationship with in your early life: your mother, stepmother, grandmother, or other significant woman. Your modeling of what these adult women did, said, thought, and valued was primarily absorbed and internalized through observation. While I'm certain I received some explicit messages such as, "Always sit with your knees together" (thanks, Grandma) or "A woman's responsibility is to make a house a home" (which I'm sure can be found in vinyl letters to put on your wall!), most of the gender messages were *caught, not taught*. Here are some examples: My extended family and church community were extra-super-over-the-Moon excited when my parents *finally* had a boy (after having three girls in a row); I learned that boy baby = more special. My mom rarely, if ever, disagreed with my dad; I learned women = not as smart as men. I saw my mom get emotionally overwhelmed often; women = emotional and irrational. My grandma had a huge closet with dozens of shoes; I figured that women = beauty. Because all of my elementary schoolteachers were female, I assumed that teacher = female. And with exposure to unhelpful, sick, and twisted messages from media and entertainment, I understood that women = objects, primarily valued for appearance and sex.

All of these beliefs I internalized were caught, not overtly taught. (Actually, I take that back—women as sex objects was caught *and* covertly taught by the larger cultural attitude.) The impact of gender on communication and relationships has filled volumes of books. But for our purposes in this book, I think it's sufficient to say that gender messages greatly matter and impact our identity, thoughts, feelings, and behaviors.

Now let's explore the messages you received when *you* were young concerning being born female.

AWARENESS EXERCISE
## What It Means to Be a Girl

Consider the following sentence stems and say whatever comes to mind:

- Ladies are…

- Girls should never say…

- Girls should always say…

- Women are primarily valued for their…

- Girls are so…

- Girls are so much better than boys at…

- Boys are so much better than girls at…

- The most important thing for girls to learn is…

- Real women always…

- Good mothers do…

- The best thing about being a girl is…

# Connecting Your Past with Your Present

No matter what type of healthy or unhealthy relationship or communication patterns you caught or were taught when you were a child, you now have the opportunity and responsibility to be more aware of them and to take ownership of your life. The beauty of being a grown-up is that you get to keep the messages that you like and challenge the gender expectations that don't serve you. As an adult woman *you* are now responsible for your life.

Your awareness of your own attachment style, differentiation level, relationship patterns, and gender messages allows you to better understand yourself. This awareness helps you move toward a more secure style as an adult. Just like with a puzzle, the more pieces of your life you put in place, the more clearly you can see the big picture. You will be able to see how you developed, and understand the impact of patterns you've inherited and the messages you've received.

Now it's your turn to put all of the pieces together and create your family relationship template. This is a chance to integrate the insights and information you've reflected on in this book thus far. Remember, there are no right or wrong answers, just authentic and inauthentic ones. Also, keep in mind that this template is a work in progress. It's flexible and will change as you discover more pieces to the puzzle. It can change as your understanding of your life story evolves.

I also want to offer a word of caution. You do not need to know *everything* about your family history. It's impossible. A frequent critique of psychotherapy is that too much time is spent going over the past! Other models of therapy focus *only* on the present and don't take historical events into account. My philosophy is somewhere in the middle: "The past is important in informing your present so you can change your future." If clients are stuck in their current life, more often than not they are stuck because they are being motivated by unprocessed, unrecognized painful situations or patterns from the past. It's helpful to identify where, in the past, they have leftover, undigested emotions so that I can help them to metabolize the emotions. In other words, I help clients access, feel, and make sense of past emotions and events in the safety of the therapeutic relationship so that they can move forward and transform their lives.

The purpose of this next exercise is to create a working template that is accurate based on what you *do* know. It requires a good amount of self-reflection.

AWARENESS EXERCISE
## Your Family Relationship Template

We've done a significant amount of self-reflecting in this chapter. Now let's do some more exploring of the self and the patterns you've discovered. The template below is available as a worksheet you can download at **http://www.newharbin ger.com/33377.**

**Family relationship patterns:**

**Family identity:**

**Emotional rules:**

**Gender messages:**

**Attachment style:** anxious / secure / avoidant

**Differentiation level:** (0–10, with 0 being low and 10 being high)

**Assertiveness approach:** hesitant / confident / guarded

We've covered a lot of ground in this chapter! You may want to take time to mull over some of these exercises, ask family members questions, and read your old journals to deepen your sense of understanding about how you got to where you are now. With careful reflection and perhaps input from others, you should have a good working model of your family relationship template. As you continue your practice of self-reflection, you will continue to gain clarity about your emotional and relational development and how it impacts your relationships today.

In the next part of the book, we'll focus on emotions and healthy ways to manage them. I will share concepts and practical tools that will help you to experience, identify, and then use your emotions as a source of valuable information. With practice, you will develop a more secure and differentiated style in your relationships, and you'll gain skills to communicate clearly and confidently.

# CHAPTER 5

# Self-Awareness: Identifying Emotions

Now that you have identified your attachment style and differentiation level, and have completed your family relationship template, you have valuable information that you can use to create and maintain more meaningful relationships—and develop personal assertiveness skills. In this chapter, you will learn how to become more connected with your emotions and how to use the information they offer to guide your assertive communication. We will also talk about the importance of integrating your feelings with your thoughts, or how to "think about feeling."

Let's start by defining emotions (which we also refer to interchangeably in this book as feelings). I find it helpful to think of emotions as E-Motions, or Energy-in-Motion. If you think of emotions as energy that *moves* you to take action or toward growth, you don't have to label them as inherently "good" or "bad." Emotions are simply *information* to help guide your interactions with others and inform you when you need to assert yourself.

Why are emotions so important? Why do they deserve your attention and energy? There are two primary reasons: First, they help you develop self-awareness. Feelings are bodily sensations that give you important cues about your subjective experience, about your likes and dislikes, your preferences. They can prompt you to seek out a closeness or distance in relationships. Feelings also prompt you take action, to assert yourself. In conjunction with your thoughts, emotions help you to know yourself—to give you information about what you like, who you like, what you want, what you need. They are key to mental health and meaningful relationships. In short, you cannot assert your thoughts, feelings, and needs until you are aware of them!

The second reason emotions matter is because they allow you to connect with others. They are key to developing empathy, which is the ability to feel *with* another person so he or she feels understood and valued. This includes being aware of and sensitive to someone else's thoughts and feelings. Empathy is at the heart of every healthy relationship, and your own level of emotional self-awareness directly impacts the amount of empathy you can experience. It's nearly impossible to recognize and validate the feelings of another if you haven't experienced them or acknowledged them within yourself.

Near the end of 2014, I had a simple yet extremely powerful empathetic exchange with a dear friend, Wendy. I was experiencing physical and emotional exhaustion. I was expressing my lack of energy and low moods to Wendy as I wondered out loud, "What is my problem?! Why am I having such a hard time right now?" Without missing a beat, Wendy replied in a tender and empathetic tone, "Of course you're having a hard time. There are so many transitions, all relating to your life's work!"

In that moment, I felt known, less alone, and more hopeful. I felt *felt*. It was a precious gift and something I will never forget.

She understood that I'd just finished writing my doctoral dissertation and was having a hard time saying good-bye to my son, who was leaving with his new wife to spend the holidays with her family. She was aware that it had been a financially stressful year for my family, and that my husband was often away on business, and I was feeling drained by both my home responsibilities and those that came with running my therapy practice. And most of all, Wendy *knew* some of the feelings of loneliness, sadness, grief, and confusion that I was experiencing. And in a very simple and yet beautiful way, she demonstrated to me not just that she cared about me but that she could literally *feel* what I felt.

This interaction helped me better understand just how meaningful empathy is in friendships. In a time of personal desperation and confusion, Wendy made me feel validated and loved. And I know enough of her background to understand that she has worked very hard to cultivate emotional awareness within herself. She allows herself to feel a range of emotions, including difficult ones, which enabled her to demonstrate to me an expression of understanding that was very much needed and appreciated. Empathy truly is the vehicle to attachment in relationships.

Your emotions are powerful tools to first understand your own self and then to forge relationships with others through exercising empathy. This level of awareness and connection can enable you to act assertively. In order to create and maintain healthy relationships as an adult, you need to integrate self-awareness and secure attachment through empathy. If you are emotionally "asleep" or cut off, it is impossible to have authentic and securely attached relationships.

Let's dive deeper into emotional self-awareness.

# Identifying Your Emotions

It's interesting that relatively little emphasis is given to helping children learn to identify and accurately label their emotions. Parents and teachers help kids understand the concept of colors and the names of shapes, letters, and numbers. But sadly, we neglect teaching young people how to name and understand their feelings. As a result, many individuals seem to still struggle with this concept as adults. As a reminder, there are six basic emotions: happiness, sadness, surprise, fear, disgust, and anger. Just like colors on a painter's palette, they can be experienced in different hues and combined to create new emotions.

In an effort to make sense of our inner experiences and use them to inform our choices and strengthen our relationships, the simple act of naming our feelings can go a long way in making them more manageable. Interpersonal neurobiologist Dan Siegel (2010) refers to this as "Name It to Tame It."

## AWARENESS EXERCISE
## Name That Feeling

Take a look at the Feelings Word List (which is also available in downloadable format at **http://www.newharbinger .com/33377**) and consider the following questions:

- Which emotions have you experienced in the last twenty-four hours?

- Which emotions on this list do you rarely experience or often aren't aware that you are experiencing? (This question applies more to an avoidant style.)

- Which feelings do you experience most often?

- Of the feelings you experience most often, are they limited to just one cluster, say "happy" or "scared"?

## Feelings Word List

| Happiness | Anger | Sadness |
|---|---|---|
| Adored | Amazed | Alone |
| Alive | Accused | Blue |
| Appreciated | Aggravated | Burdened |
| Cheerful | Angry | Depressed |
| Ecstatic | Bitter | Devastated |
| Excited | Cross | Disappointed |
| Glad | Defensive | Discouraged |
| Grateful | Frustrated | Grief-stricken |
| Hopeful | Furious | Gloomy |
| Jolly | Hostile | Heartbroken |
| Jovial | Impatient | Hopeless |
| Joyful | Infuriated | Let down |
| Loved | Insulted | Lonely |
| Merry | Jaded | Melancholy |
| Optimistic | Offended | Miserable |
| Pleased | Ornery | Neglected |
| Satisfied | Outraged | Pessimistic |
| Tender | Pestered | Remorseful |
| Terrific | Rebellious | Resentful |
| Thankful | Resistant | Solemn |
| Uplifted | Scorned | |
| Warm | Spiteful | |
| | Testy | |
| | Used | |
| | Vengeful | |
| | Violated | |

| Fear | Surprise | Disgust |
|------|----------|---------|
| Afraid | Astonished | Ashamed |
| Alarmed | Curious | Embarrassed |
| Anxious | Delighted | Exposed |
| Bashful | Enchanted | Guilty |
| Cautious | Exhilarated | Ignored |
| Fearful | Impressed | Inadequate |
| Frightened | Incredulous | Incompetent |
| Haunted | Inquisitive | Inept |
| Helpless | Mystified | Inferior |
| Hesitant | Playful | Inhibited |
| Horrified | Replenished | Insignificant |
| Insecure | Shocked | Sick |
| Lost | Startled | Squashed |
| Nervous | Stunned | Stupid |
| Petrified | | Ugly |
| Puzzled | | Unaccepted |
| Reserved | | |
| Sheepish | | |
| Tearful | | |
| Threatened | | |
| Uncomfortable | | |
| Useless | | |

Since the simple act of naming or labeling an emotion makes it more manageable and decreases its intensity, accurately identifying your feelings is an important part of self-awareness. It also helps with self-soothing, or emotional management. This chart can help you begin to label and fine-tune your emotional awareness. I've had several clients and other therapists suggest that clients put this chart on their fridge or desk as a reminder to periodically tune in to their emotions, label them, and choose whether those emotions need to be shared. I still refer to this list when I can't quite put my finger on what I'm experiencing.

## Primary and Secondary Emotions

Working with clients in private practice, I've noticed that some emotions are more readily accessible than others. We are often more likely to directly acknowledge and express comfortable or pleasant emotions and to suppress those that are more painful or vulnerable such as shame, anger, or fear. Some in the field of psychology frame this as a distinction between primary and secondary emotions. A *primary emotion* is the one that is felt *first* (usually a vulnerable or powerless emotion) while a *secondary emotion* is one that is felt *most,* or expressed openly and visibly. The secondary emotion's purpose is to protect our vulnerability.

To better understand this principle, I like to consider the "ocean-emotion" analogy: If you were to look at the surface of an ocean, you may see some traces of life: a few seagulls above, a boat off in the distance, and, if you're lucky, a dolphin jumping out of the water. But, as you deep-sea divers know (and from what I can gather from National Geographic Channel), the real heart of it all is *underneath* the surface, that is, where the rich abundance of plants and animals reside. There are coral reefs, millions of fish, whales, sharks, dolphins, rays, snails, sea anemone, sea crabs, kelp, microbes, and more (cue music "Under the Sea" from Disney's *The Little Mermaid*).

While the secondary emotion is what's readily apparent and overtly expressed, the primary emotion is the core of your experience, or the emotion that's in charge. For example, if a child runs into the street, her mother may yell at her in frustration. Her body language, tone of voice, and words may convey anger (which would be the secondary emotion), but this merely covers her true feelings, which would likely be fear for the life of her daughter (the primary emotion).

Primary emotions often show up in my clinical practice disguised as criticism, blaming, and irritability. In fact, come to think of it, that's often how they show up in my own life!

My youngest daughter, Macy, is a collector. Everything is special to her, and, as a result, her bedroom has been a cluttered mess for...I don't know how long. One evening, when she was eight, I had turned out her bedroom light and lain next to her to snuggle. I said, "Sis, you've got to do something about this room. It's not acceptable. It's way too messy." She got a bit defensive and said, "It's just like you say about your office, Mom—it's messy but you still know where everything is." I was busted! Brushing off her tangential yet true comment, I continued, "Okay, tomorrow you *have* to get this room picked up! No excuses." The conversation soon escalated, and she ended up teary; I ended up frustrated and walked out of her room envisioning her story being featured in a TV episode of *Hoarders* in twenty years.

During the next twenty-four hours, I thought a lot about our conversation and why her room was such a big trigger for me. Was it really just her room? Why was I so quickly annoyed, irritated, and intense about that one thing (especially when I obviously needed to organize and clean my office!)? As I thought about secondary and primary emotions, I was able to get to the primary emotion driving my conversation with Macy. My vulnerable emotion was fear. I was afraid that I was a bad parent because I wasn't teaching my daughter how to be organized, how to take care of her things, how to clean her room. That's part of being a "good mom," right? Not coincidently, these are areas of weakness for me. While I can organize thoughts and ideas and words, I have a really hard time organizing tangible "stuff."

A day or two after our conversation, I approached Macy calmly and tenderly and offered an apology. "Macy, you know that talk we had about your messy room a couple of nights ago?" She nodded. "I need to apologize. It really wasn't about your room. It's about me feeling scared that I'm not a good mom, that I'm failing because I'm not teaching you how to be orga- nized and take care of things. I was so upset because it's some- thing I'm not very good at—keeping things orderly and organized. Our conversation was really about me, not about your room. Will you forgive me?" She nodded and gave me a big hug. Identifying my primary emotion allowed me to share it with my daughter in a way that brought us closer instead of creating distance.

Now the story doesn't end here. And this next part is almost too good to be true. But it is true...and awesome! You know what Macy did after my apology? She cleaned her room, filled up a few bags of stuff she wanted to give away, and organized the rest immaculately. And the best part is that she has kept it that way! It was definitely a highlight in my parenting book. Not only did my vulnerability inspire my daughter to clean her chronically messy room, but sharing it with her allowed me to feel very deeply that I am a good mother. Although I am not the best at teaching Macy how to organize, I am good at teach- ing her how to feel and express difficult emotions.

Distinguishing between primary and secondary emotions can be difficult for many people, as it can be painful or uncom- fortable to deal with raw, vulnerable emotion. In the messy room story, it would have been a lot more comfortable for me to remain indignant that Macy's room was the problem and that I was absolutely justified in being irritated and frustrated with her. Nevertheless, it's an important skill to practice in order to cultivate greater emotional awareness, to recognize what you want and what you need, and to clearly communicate with others. For an exercise to help you with this, visit **http://www .newharbinger.com/33377**.

## Sorting Thoughts and Feelings

One important distinction relating to emotional awareness is the ability to separate feelings and thoughts (this ties in to an aspect of differentiation). Confusion may exist because feelings and thoughts are interconnected and mutually influence one another. Though they try, researchers have yet to determine which, if any, come first. Since babies can feel and take purposeful action before they think with words, I tend to lean toward emotions preceding thoughts. If I had to choose between chicken or the egg...I choose the egg.

Even though in your day-to-day living you experience thoughts and feelings concurrently and connectedly, it can be helpful to sort through them separately in order to inform your next step and to articulate your internal experience to others. You might think of thoughts versus feelings using the common metaphor: thoughts refer to activity and logic taking place in the mind, whereas emotions and feelings reside in the heart. There may be confusion and/or relationship blips when you accidentally express a thought as if you were expressing a feeling. For example, saying, "I feel that you are trying to manipulate me" is problematic because it is actually a thought, not a feeling. Just because you say the word "feeling" doesn't mean you're actually stating a feeling. Look at the following template for a more accurate way of teasing out a thought from a feeling in order to express yourself more effectively:

I feel _____ when you _____ because I think _____.
    (emotion word)     (other's specific behavior)     (your thought)

We will revisit this same sentence stem in more depth in chapter 8 as a helpful tool for assertive communication. But for now, you can play around with it as a way to sort through your feelings and thoughts.

## Emotional Intelligence

Many seem to believe that trusting our head over our heart is the best way to live and make decisions. The concept of *emotional intelligence*, however, helps us understand that both thoughts *and* emotions can help us gain insight and clarity, and make choices that will lead to our happiness and fulfillment. Emotional intelligence refers to cohesively bringing thoughts and emotions together. It can be seen as the successful combination of the two—that is, *thinking* about your emotions. Developed by Salovey and Mayer (1990), the official definition of emotional intelligence is "a type of social intelligence that involves the ability to monitor one's own and other's emotions, to discriminate among them, and to use that information to guide one's thinking and actions" (189). In other words, you begin by cultivating an awareness of your emotions, then you develop the skill of discerning them from one another and extracting value and meaning before finally *acting* on them. Emotional intelligence is a prerequisite for assertiveness to take place.

As I reflect on my own life, I can see a direct correlation between decisions and steps made that were informed by both my thoughts *and* emotions. My career beginnings exemplify this: When I started working on my master of social work degree, my husband and I had already become parents to our first child, Tanner. Since both of us come from large (or extra-large) families, we knew that we wanted our child to have siblings. We talked, prayed, and pondered about whether to wait until I graduated (which would be three more years) until we had another child, or whether we wanted to add another child to our already full lives. Being a mom, working as a performing songwriter and part-time social service worker, *and* going to school was already a lot to manage. My thoughts and everyone I talked to told me to wait until I finished my degree; it would be too much for me to have another baby during graduate school. But my intuition, my "gut," informed me that now was the time to bring another child into our family. When my thoughts and emotions are conflicting, more often than not, my emotions trump my thoughts. We had a beautiful baby daughter, Madeline, in between semesters during my second year of graduate school. Looking back, I can see that that was the best decision for me and for our family (how I actually pulled that off with good grades and happy children is the subject for another book!).

While the theory of emotional intelligence relates to thinking about and discerning your *own* feelings, it goes beyond just you: to be truly emotionally intelligent, you have to have an awareness of others' emotions too. You are tuned in to and sensitive toward others' experiences, and you use this information to help you carefully navigate your interactions while still paying heed to your desires and needs.

In summary, awareness of your feelings as sources of information is at the heart of developing self-awareness, a necessary component of acting assertively. You cannot act assertively if you aren't tuned in to your internal experiences and cues. The ability to recognize and accurately label your internal states helps lower the intensity of your emotions and makes them more manageable. The continual expansion of language to name and describe the nuances of your emotional experience allows you to expand your self-knowledge *and* your ability to experience empathy toward others. Distinguishing thoughts and feelings, as you learned to do in this chapter, will help you clarify the messages you want to communicate to others. And throughout it all, empathy will be the bridge to creating the securely attached relationships that are central to assertiveness.

In the next chapter, we will build upon these concepts and look at specific mindfulness-based practices that you can incorporate in your life to effectively manage your emotions. You will also learn how the practices of self-compassion and shame resilience can create a balanced relationship with yourself, so you can more effectively communicate, or assert, your wants and needs.

# CHAPTER 6

# Self-Soothing: Mindfulness and Emotional Management

Now that you understand the significance of emotions, let's shift gears to exactly *how* to integrate self-awareness practices and skills into your life so that you can harness their power and create positive changes. Tapping in to your emotions may sound simple, but it can actually be a complex process to truly understand what and how you are feeling. Equally important is how to effectively *manage* your emotions (particularly difficult ones)—that is, learning to control them instead of allowing them to control you.

Read on to discover some useful strategies developed by experts to help you really tune in to your internal experiences and then to manage them.

## Practicing Mindfulness

We've discussed the importance of being aware, or mindful, of your emotions. Now we will talk about mindfulness as a *practice*, not just as an idea. Mindfulness involves regularly quieting yourself and observing yourself, focusing on your thoughts and feelings, noticing your bodily sensations—touch, pressure, smell, sounds, sights—during the present moment. According to Jon Kabat-Zinn, "*mindfulness* means paying attention in a particular way; on purpose, in the present moment, and nonjudgmentally" (1994, 4). The concept of not judging our feelings can be particularly difficult, as we are often prone to evaluating them.

I once spoke with a thirty-five-year-old woman whose experience illustrates the importance of being nonjudgmental toward one's emotions. Diane was greatly distressed due to her best friend's upcoming marriage; she was sad that her relationship with her friend would change and also deeply pained that she herself was not yet married, as Diane had always imagined that by her age she would have a husband and children. Unfortunately, Diane compounded her own suffering because she felt guilty about her emotions; she thought that feeling these things meant she wasn't happy for her friend. I encouraged her to not judge her emotions as "bad" and reassured her that they didn't mean she didn't love her friend. By allowing herself to experience difficult emotions *and* hold space for all of her feelings (without deeming them wrong or inappropriate), Diane could honor her own pain, grieve her unmet expectation, *and* celebrate her friend's happy occasion.

The practice of mindfulness allows you to let thoughts, feelings, and sensations flow through you without trying to change them in any way, and without judging your experiences. Though it is really quite a simple concept, this exercise takes focus and practice, as it is so different from the way our brains normally operate. We very often find ourselves living in the past or in the future, but practicing mindfulness challenges you to experience yourself in the present. This is a continual process of knowing yourself at a deeper level and, with time, this practice can strengthen your self-differentiation and also guide your assertiveness.

Remember in chapter 1 how we talked about the five components of assertiveness? The second component is to cultivate *self-awareness* of your thoughts, feelings, needs, and wants; the practice of mindfulness is designed to help you do just that.

---

AWARENESS EXERCISE
## Two-Minute Mindful Breathing

Sit in a comfortable position and close your eyes. Focus on your breath. Without trying to change anything, just notice your breath. Notice if you are breathing shallowly or deeply… or if you are breathing slowly or rapidly. Get curious about your breath. As you continue to be aware of your breathing, you may find your mind moving away from your breath toward other sounds or noises in the room. Notice where your mind goes. When your mind wanders, thank it for its awareness and, without judgment, slowly bring your focus back to your breathing.

---

# Finding Your Wise Mind

Although your emotions are some of the most important pieces of knowledge you have to inform your relationships, assertiveness, and life, they can sometimes be difficult to understand and navigate. Once you are in touch with your feelings, how can you utilize them for energy and action without being overwhelmed? The ability to create a healthy working distance from your emotions is a process, not a static state to be achieved. The goal is to be able to separate thoughts and feelings in your mind, and then act from the place where they overlap. In dialectical behavior therapy, developed by Dr. Marsha Linehan (1993), this is known as accessing the "wise mind." Linehan posits that the "emotion mind" occurs when we are being controlled by our current emotional states, and "reasonable mind" is when our thoughts and actions are focused solely on logic and objectivity.

To illustrate Linehan's reasoning, let's say you are tired and mad at your coworker, so you decide to stay in bed and not go to work one day; this is emotion mind at work. However, reasonable mind would say, "You shouldn't miss work just because you're upset. You should be responsible and act like a grownup." Wise mind enters at the junction where reasonable mind and emotion mind overlap. For example, wise mind might say something like, "I know you're mad and you're tired and you don't want to go to work today. Even though not going to work would feel like a relief, that's probably not a good idea because you enjoy your job and you want to keep your job."

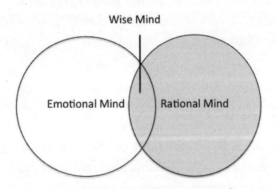

Figure 4. Wise Mind

Let's consider the case of Judith, a lovely, smart, fortysomething wife and mother of three children who'd come to therapy for depression and relationship struggles. After some initial counseling, it became evident that making and keeping close female friendships had been difficult and painful during most of her adulthood. Judith came in for one session tense and anxious after hearing that her closest friend had broken a confidence and shared details about her teen daughter's battle with an eating disorder. She had a history of oversensitivity to any kind of betrayal and was flooded with feelings of fear, anger, and hurt.

During the session, I asked Judith to give voice to her emotion mind. She had no problem launching into a rant about how she couldn't trust anyone. "It feels just like it was growing up, when my mom and sister would talk about me and criticize me. I am never going to talk to this friend again. She had me fooled! I thought she was a true friend, but I was wrong."

Next, I invited Judith to speak from her rational, reasonable mind. Even though she appeared very collected and poised, this part of the session was a lot harder for her. "My reasonable mind is saying that there is a slight possibility that she didn't do it intentionally or share my daughter's eating disorder to hurt me or to ruin our friendship. We've been friends for so long. I hate to see it end like this. Maybe she did it because she was concerned? I think I'll go and tell her how I feel—that she had no right to share something that I asked her not to!"

Then we transitioned to giving voice to her wise mind. Judith began, "Well, we have been friends for years. I am so hurt that I'm tempted to never speak to her again, but our friendship deserves at least a conversation about what has happened. I know that my family-of-origin stuff—feeling betrayed by my mom and sister—is getting all mixed up in this situation, too." Through using the practice of wise mind, Judith was able to integrate her intense emotions with her rational thoughts to find a more balanced response to the situation. She was also able to modulate her emotions and plan a proactive instead of reactive course of action to talk to her friend about the situation.

AWARENESS EXERCISE

## Connecting to Your Wise Mind

Think of a recent time when you had an intense emotional response to something that occurred in a relationship (it could be with a spouse, family member, friend, coworker, or even a stranger). What did your emotional mind say? What did your reasonable mind say? Were you able to see both perspectives of the issue to integrate your emotions and reasons into wise mind? If not, and if you could go back in time, what would your wise mind say?

# Cultivating Self-Compassion

We frequently hear talk of self-esteem, or a positive evaluation of oneself. This (sometimes overused) term has made its way into mainstream vocabulary, and we often speak about it like it is the most important aspect of ourselves. Some have argued that popular culture has fallen in love with the concept of self-esteem and believe that low self-esteem contributes to many of our social ills, like bullying, violence, and dropping out of school.

Self-esteem is defined by the degree to which you judge yourself as competent in the parts of life that are important to you (Neff and Vonk 2009). It is based on self-evaluation and on how you believe others evaluate you; for this reason, it's often comparative in nature. The concept of self-esteem is rooted in the idea of being "better than average," which often leads to inflated evaluations or perceptions of yourself. In other words, to be deemed average, satisfactory, or sufficient is not "good enough" for high self-esteem.

Self-compassion, on the other hand, is not based in a positive self-evaluation or how you see yourself. Rather, it is a type of open-hearted awareness and way of responding to your own suffering that allows room for all aspects of personal experience, including failure and pain.

Self-compassion researcher and psychologist Dr. Kristin Neff suggests, "It is certainly better to feel worthy and proud than worthless and ashamed. More problematic is what people do to get and keep a sense of high self-esteem" (2011, 2). Given that self-esteem is often obtained from specific areas of life such as appearance, school performance, athletic ability, and popularity, self-esteem has become linked to specific outcomes in these areas (Neff 2011). Basing your self-esteem on performance or evaluation can make it fragile and unstable, and lead you to overfocus on the fear of what might happen if your evaluation or status is threatened (Kernis 2005). (This idea connects back to the ladder/field analogy from chapter 3—remember the ranking on one end and the linking/connecting on the other end of the continuum?)

I've witnessed this in my clinical practice with many teenage and young adult athletes who report high self-esteem as long as they are excelling in their given sport. But when a gymnast breaks an ankle, a soccer player takes one too many headers and suffers a concussion, or a football player is benched for poor grades, the once-high self-esteem quickly plummets because the high evaluation is gone. "What reason do I have to get up in the morning? What makes me special now?" are questions I've heard from tearful athletes who have devoted their efforts to a sport that they are no longer able to play, temporarily or permanently.

I've also seen this loss of self-worth in women who have built their self-esteem contingent on how their children "turn out": their children's good behavior, good grades, popularity, or entrance into an Ivy League college. Because self-esteem is connected to the positive evaluation of one's child, if a child is evaluated as "average" on a standardized test, leaves the family's faith, becomes a junkie, or flunks out of Harvard, the mother's self-esteem, happiness, and sanity hinges on things that are beyond her control. If your self-esteem is linked to others' behavior, even to your children's behavior, you are giving control over how you see and evaluate yourself to someone else. Self-compassion, on the other hand, is solely in your control and always available to you.

Some self-evaluations are based on entrenched patterns of interpreting yourself in a negative light (fact vs. story). For example, if as a child you were told over and over again that you weren't smart, you've likely internalized that belief about yourself and may interpret current situations through this "I'm not smart" lens. That is a self-evaluation based on your thoughts. To be clear, I am *not* saying that self-esteem or your self-evaluation doesn't matter. Of course they do. Your thoughts have an impact on your emotions and behavior. However, I believe that there is a concept that is more helpful when it comes to emotional management.

In 2003, Dr. Neff turned the notion of self-esteem on its head when she introduced the refreshing concept of *self-compassion*. While others had examined compassionate behavior toward the self, Neff refined the idea and operationalized the definition and measurement of self-compassion. While self-esteem is based on your *cognitive evaluation* of any given part of yourself or your life, self-compassion is based on how you *respond to* your own suffering.

Neff asserts that, when compared to self-esteem, self-compassion is associated with greater emotional resilience, more accurate self-concepts, increased caring, and fewer narcissistic tendencies. She speaks of self-compassion in terms of kindness toward yourself (having kind and warm responses to your own imperfections and suffering) and common humanity (recognizing that you are not alone in your experience of disappointment, pain, and suffering). Neff makes it clear that self-compassion is *not* self-pity or chronically feeling sorry for yourself. It's also not the same as self-indulgence (i.e., I'm sad about being fired, so I'm going to sit on the couch for the week and eat ice cream three meals a day). Instead, it is being aware of our emotions and responding compassionately—just like we would respond to another's pain.

Imagine that a good friend wasn't hired for her high-paying dream job and came to you in tears expressing hopelessness and fear. What would be a compassionate response? If it were me, I'd give her a big hug, invite her to sit down on the couch, and encourage her to tell me all about it. I'd let her cry. I'd validate her pain and disappointment by saying things like, "Oh, that is so disappointing. I know how much you hoped this job would work out. I'm here for you."

Now imagine that you just found out that you weren't hired for your high-paying dream job. How would you respond to your *own* hopelessness and disappointment about not being hired for the job? I might respond with a mix of compassion and criticism, saying things like, "Yes, this is disappointing, but did you *really* think they'd consider you for this job? I'm sure there are a lot of people who are more highly qualified. Maybe your expectations are just too high when it comes to employment. Ugh!" I would likely say things to myself that I would never say to my friend. I also wouldn't think about giving myself a hug or touching my arm in a comforting way.

Most people find it easier to feel and act compassionately toward others than to their own difficult experiences.

*"I'm supposed to be the strong one in my family."*

*"I was taught that it's not okay to cry. Crying is for sissies."*

*"I am so sad about the death of my son, but I was just taught to 'soldier on' and get back to work."*

I've heard these phrases come from clients who are dealing with significant struggles and pain. To me, they indicate that we don't give ourselves permission to grieve, to be sad, or to be imperfect. But do we not allow for these things for others when they are in emotional pain? My hope for you is that, with practice, you'll extend the same compassion to yourself as you extend to others.

## AWARENESS EXERCISE
### Practicing Self-Compassion

Think of a recent situation when you've felt pain of any kind. It could be a physical injury or a relationship injury. It might be an unexpected loss such as unemployment, a break up, or the untimely death of a loved on. Now, reflect on the following questions:

- What did I tell myself about my pain?

- Was my self-talk nurturing or was it critical?

- Did I validate my suffering or minimize it?

- How did I behave toward myself when I was hurting?

- Was I able to provide nurturing, comfort, and validation to myself?

Now, think of a child you know. It may be your own child, a neighbor, extended relative, or the child of a friend. Place this beloved child in the previous scenario, experiencing a similar pain, and reflect on the following questions:

- What would I say to her? Would my words be nurturing or lean toward criticism and judgment?

- How would I behave?

- Would I validate her suffering with empathy or would I minimize her pain?

- How is my imagined response to a child's suffering different or similar to how I respond to my own pain?

All attachment styles can benefit from the practice of self-compassion. If you have an anxious attachment style, self-compassion can help you self-soothe and validate your own experience without feeling so dependent on validation and comfort from others. If you have a securely attached style, a self-compassion practice will help you validate the emotional ups and downs that occur as a natural part of life. For avoid-antly attached women, self-compassion will help you acknowledge, access, and connect to your own suffering (and joy) instead of distancing from painful experiences or denying it in order to cope.

What does self-compassion have to do with assertiveness? The practice of self-compassion allows you to be aware, to tune in, to be mindful of your experiences, and to provide comfort and self-nurturing when you need it. That is, to think and *act* in comforting and compassionate ways toward yourself. The self-compassion process helps validate and soothe pain enough to let it teach and guide you to your actions. This is the healthy distance from your emotions we discussed in chapter 4. The ability to soothe and comfort yourself allows you to move toward identifying your wants and needs from others and informs your requests of others. It's also part of differentiation because it enables you to comfort yourself instead of solely relying on others to soothe you.

Since I first learned about self-compassion a couple of years ago, I have made it a practice—and I can attest that it works. It feels *really* good to comfort yourself and take care of yourself, though slightly uncomfortable at first. During the process of writing my doctoral dissertation I experienced insecurities about my competence, my capability, and my worthiness. More than once (okay, if I'm really honest with myself, it's like ten times) I broke down in tears, overwhelmed with feelings of self-doubt, inadequacy, and fear, and vowing that I was going to drop out of my program. I found myself saying things to myself that I would *never* say to another person! My self-talk was something along the lines of, "Who are *you* to think that you can write a scholarly document and actually have it pass as some kind of original contribution to the field of marriage and family therapy? You don't have what it takes. You've never been the smart one in your family. You're the social one, the songwriter, the therapist, but definitely *not* a scholar. Who are you kidding?" Luckily, I became aware of what I was saying to myself and saw it as an opportunity to practice self-compassion. I shifted into a mode of self-compassion instead of self-contempt.

I started stroking my arm softly, like I have done hundreds of times to my children when they were struggling, saying to myself, "Julie, this is really, *really* hard. You have taken on something that is challenging you in completely new ways. You are having to shift how you view yourself and your capabilities. Of course it's bringing up feelings of inadequacy and thoughts that you're not good enough. Remember the stories you've heard from other friends and colleagues who've completed their PhDs? They *all* had times when they wanted to walk away; when they feared they weren't up to the challenge. You are not alone. You can do this. You have taken on and worked through other difficult, scary, and vulnerable risks and you're still here. It's okay to feel overwhelmed. I am here for you." I value being present and empathetic to others, and it felt so comforting—so satisfying—to be there for *me*.

# Developing Shame Resilience

While it's crucial to listen to your feelings, there is one in particular that can sabotage healthy relationships and hijack your emotional well-being: *shame*. Shame is the deeply painful and vulnerable experience of not feeling good enough or worthy of love (Brown 2012). It can dominate your other emotions and paralyze your ability to change—it's difficult to practice mindful awareness and self-compassion when you are experiencing yourself as a bad person. Shame can kill your willingness to act assertively because you feel like you don't deserve to have your needs attended to.

One of the key things to understand about shame is that *everyone* experiences it. Regularly. It is truly a universal emotion. Shame is so common because it is elicited by a variety of different scenarios: failure, mistakes, abuse, rejection. Arguably, the biggest trigger of shame is anything that challenges the way you want to view yourself and be perceived by others (Ferguson, Eyre, and Ashbaker 2000). Basically, the answers to the questions "How do I want to view myself and be viewed by others?" and "How do I *not* want to be viewed?" give you a clear picture about what threatens your ideal identity and triggers shame.

I want to see myself and to be thought of as someone who is inclusive and open-minded, and this is part of my "ideal identity." When I think that I am being close-minded or silencing someone else's voice, I can slide into feeling shame. Another example of my ideal identity, and a common one for women with children, is that I want to see myself and have others view me as a "good mother." So, if I think that I have been working too much and have not been as attentive to my children (bad mother), I am taking on an unwanted identity and susceptible to feelings of shame. Because we all have wanted and unwanted identities, and because we are all human and will not be able to live up to our self-expectations 100 percent of the time, experiencing shame is inevitable.

In recent years, Dr. Brené Brown has conducted extensive research on shame that gives us valuable insight into how to deal with this painful experience. She explains that shame needs three things to grow and fester: secrecy, silence, and judgment. According to her research, *empathy* is the antidote to shame.

Brown's model of shame resilience offers four steps to combating shame:

1. Recognize when we are feeling shame and understand its triggers.

2. Develop practicing critical awareness, or normalizing our shame, by knowing that everyone experiences shame and by seeing the bigger picture.

3. Reach out to trusted relationships for support (which is more natural if you have a secure attachment style).

4. Tell our stories and share shame with someone we trust to respond compassionately and empathetically. This helps us find a way through our feelings of shame (Brown 2012).

For women, shame often feels like "a sticky, complex spiderweb of layered, conflicting, and competing expectations that dictate exactly who we should be, what we should be, how we should be" (Brown 2012, 87). As an example, let's look at Leann, a woman in her midthirties who outwardly appears to have a spectacular life. She is ambitious, kind, beautiful, and smart, and she has the attention of many men. Inwardly, however, Leann experiences debilitating shame. Both of her parents had substance addictions, and though Leann hasn't had to fight the same demons, she feels unworthy of love. Sadly, she believes that if anyone gets close enough to her to truly know her, he or she wouldn't want her because of her family baggage. This has caused her to resist intimate relationships and miss out on opportunities to connect with others for fear that if they *really knew her* they would certainly not love and accept her and her imperfections. While on the outside she looks well put together, she is trapped in a shame web, attempting to look beautiful, work hard, and not let anyone down while hiding her own pain.

## AWARENESS EXERCISE
## Recognizing Shame and Its Triggers

Now that you have an understanding of shame, let's look closer into what shame feels like for you. Think of an experience when you felt shame (when you felt *defective* and *unworthy* as a person, not just when you made a mistake).

- What "ideal identity" or "unwanted identity" triggered your shame?

- Where in your body did you experience shame? (Dr. Brown has described it as a "warm wash.")

- How would you describe its color, texture, temperature, shape, or weight (or any other characteristic)?

- When you felt shame, what was your initial behavioral response? Did you want to leave a situation? Did you want to crawl in a hole? Did you reach out to someone, or did you want to be alone?

Thankfully, through working with a therapist and reaching out to close friends, Leann has become more aware of her shame and has used her difficult family experiences to relate to others through empathy. These friends have, in turn, reached back to support her. She is not miraculously "fixed" of her struggles, but she has learned techniques to move through shame and is improving in her ability to create and maintain meaningful connections through developing resilience.

---

AWARENESS EXERCISE
## Sharing Your Shame

Using the same scenario from the previous exercise, answer the following questions:

- Did you share your shame experience with a trusted friend or family member? Why or why not?

- If you spoke about your shame, how did the other person respond to your disclosure?

- If you didn't share your shame at the time, can you identify someone with whom you could share your experience?

- Would you be willing to talk about your shame next time?

---

Practicing shame resilience can prevent you from being controlled by shame or from spending unnecessary time trying to *avoid* feeling it. Like mindfulness, wise mind, and self-compassion, shame resilience is a practice that becomes more natural over time. What I *don't* want to happen is for you to feel shame about having shame, or not being shame-resilient enough. It is a practice. It is a process. It will take time.

# Separating Meaning from Fact

One of my favorite quotes is "Pain is inevitable. Suffering is optional" from author Haruki Murakami (Murakami and Gabriel 2008, vii). Keep this idea in mind as we conclude this chapter by exploring how our thoughts might be causing us to suffer unnecessarily. The next awareness practice will ask you to really examine your thoughts. It's perhaps more challenging than the other exercises I've shared so far, but it can be a very powerful game-changer on the path to becoming more assertive. Therapists call it "cognitive reframing," which is just a fancy way to describe something we do all day, every day, without much conscious thought: inferring meaning and messages from facts and events in our lives. We draw conclusions about human nature from our interactions with others. But people can find themselves in trouble when they make assumptions that may or may not be true, and sometimes these beliefs that go unchallenged can limit your growth. So it may be necessary to *cognitively reframe* our experiences to draw more accurate meaning and conclusions from them.

Let me start by sharing a memory from my upbringing: One Sunday morning when I was a teenager, my siblings and I—all nine of us—piled into the car with our parents to attend church. During the meeting, my dad received a distressing call from our trusted neighbor, Gerry. "You and Linda need to come home, Lex. Your house has been burglarized!" Our home alarm had gone off, and Gerry was standing by as the police inspected the scene. Expecting the worse, my mom and dad raced home. When they arrived and walked into the door, my dad looked around to assess the damage done, then said, "Yep. Just the way we left it!" Turns out that eleven people rushing to get dressed, fed, and out the door on time can create a mess that could easily pass for a ransacking! And the alarm? Our family dog, McBarker, had set it off.

I share this funny account because it shows a distinction between something that happened and someone's *perception*, or story, about what happened. The facts remained the same: my family's house was a complete disaster, but the stories assigned to them were different; our neighbor assumed that we'd been robbed (and I don't blame her one bit!), whereas we understood the true reason for the disarray.

So why does all this matter? And what does it have to do with emotional management and assertiveness? The idea is that we can easily assume that our emotions and our thoughts are facts, without questioning them. For instance, some individuals carry emotional pain not from an actual event but from their *interpretation* of what occurred at the event. For example, one individual I worked with grew up believing that the severe abuse he experienced as a child at the hands of his parents was because he had done something wrong and, therefore, was not worthy of the love of his parents (or anyone else). It took psychotherapy for him to challenge his long-held belief, to challenge the story that he had been telling himself, and to come to understand that the abuse he experienced didn't have to be a reflection on himself. Only then could he believe it was instead an unfortunate result of his parents' severe mental illness going untreated. While the meaning he made out of the abuse is common to survivors of childhood trauma and made perfect sense given his experience, he was allowing his belief that the abuse rendered him unlovable to prevent him from forming meaningful relationships.

Cognitive reframing can apply to dramatic situations like the one mentioned above, but it is also relevant to more common, everyday occurrences. If a good friend doesn't return your phone call for a week, you may be tempted to create a story that she is ignoring you or is being unkind, whereas the truth may be that she has been sick, having phone problems, or has simply gotten way behind on checking her messages. Separating the facts from the meaning we assign them can help you feel empowered to change the story (if necessary). We don't often challenge our thoughts. And here's the clincher: Just because you think something, or have a deeply ingrained belief, *doesn't mean it's true.*

I love the work of Byron Katie, a formerly chronically depressed woman who developed a theory of self-inquiry known as "The Work" that helps us examine our thoughts (Katie and Mitchell 2002) and determine whether they are serving us or causing suffering. Katie suggests that *all* suffering is a result of believing your own thoughts. So if something is causing you emotional pain, consider examining it and seeing whether the thoughts you believe are perpetuating your suffering. We can learn how to change the narrative in ways that help us instead of continually hurt us. There is peace and freedom that comes from breaking out of a cycle of buying into stories or assumptions that don't serve you and impede your personal development and relationships.

Katie has formulated four questions to help you examine and challenge your habitual thought patterns. They are:

1. Is the thought true?

2. Can I absolutely know that it's true?

3. How do I react—what happens—when I believe the thought?

4. Who would I be without the thought? (Katie and Mitchell 2002)

The questions aren't about *changing* your thoughts but about *examining* them. To do this, Katie suggests that you answer the four questions, pause, then do a "turnaround"—determine the opposite of your initial thought and then run through the questions again. After the second run-through, decide if the turnaround answers are true, or truer, than your original answers.

Here's an example of the four questions in action. Rita and Jen met five years ago at an accounting firm where they worked. Since then, they had been through a lot together: Rita's divorce, Jen and her husband's struggle with infertility, and the day-to-day job stresses they shared. For the past month, Rita sensed Jen pulling away and not seeking her out as often, declining Rita's social invitations, and spending more time with Shalise, another coworker. Rita thought to herself, "Well, I guess Jen doesn't care about our friendship anymore."

Let's walk with Rita through the four questions examining the thought "Jen doesn't care about our friendship anymore."

1. Is it true? *I don't know.*

2. Can I absolutely know it's true? *No.*

3. How do I react—what happens—when I believe the thought? *I give Jen the cold shoulder, feel hesitant to reach out to others, and feel a sense of distrust.*

4. Who would I be without the thought? *I would be more open to Jen. I would ask her if there's something bothering her, and I'd feel more emotionally open.*

Now for the turnaround: Rita picked an opposite thought—"Jen cares about our friendship"—and runs through the questions again.

1. Is it true? *Maybe.*

2. Can I absolutely know it's true? *No.*

3. How do I react—what happens—when I believe the thought? *I remain open to the friendship. I feel confident that although the friendship may be evolving it's not ending. I remain emotionally open to developing friendships with others.*

4. Who would I be without the thought? *I would be where I am now: Feeling rejected and thinking Jen doesn't care about me.*

Either thought—the initial one or its opposite—could be true, but now Rita gets to decide which thought is serving her. We often get caught up in whether our thought is right or not. However, in relationships, even when you openly ask, you may never know if the other person is telling the truth. What this exercise demonstrates is the power of examining our own automatic assumptions and deciding which serve us and help us become who we want to become. In the Rita and Jen example, believing the thought "Jen still cares about our friendship" helped Rita move to a place where she could remain open in her relationship with Jen. Doing the turnaround allowed Rita to entertain the thought that the relationship was changing, helped her remain emotionally open to other relationships, and fostered more positive emotions.

## AWARENESS EXERCISE

# Are Your Thoughts Helping or Hurting You?

Think of a relationship situation that is causing you pain. Now identify one simple thought that you have noticed either about yourself or the other person. (A worksheet for this exercise is available for download at **http://www.newharbin ger.com/33377.**)

The thought I want to examine is _____.

Now answer the following questions:

1. Is it true?

2. Can I absolutely know it's true?

3. How do I react—what happens—when I believe the thought?

4. Who would I be without the thought?

Now turn the thought around to its opposite. Write it down.

My opposite thought is _____.

Now answer the same four questions with your opposite thought:

1. Is it true?

2. Can I absolutely know it's true?

3. How do I react—what happens—when I believe the thought?

4. Who would I be without the thought?

Which thought—your original or its opposite—feels more truthful? Explore which thought inspires you to act in ways that feel better to you and that serve your relationship. Remember, the questions aren't about *changing* your thoughts but about *examining* them.

Now that you've been introduced to several self-soothing skills, let's revisit attachment styles and explore how these emotional management skills can help each style.

## Emotional Management Skills and Attachment Style

While the self-soothing practices outlined in this chapter—mindfulness, wise mind, self-compassion, shame resilience, and separating fact from the story—have been shown to have positive physical and emotional effects in general, they also have unique value for each attachment style. If you lean toward an anxious attachment style, these practices can help you create a stronger sense of peace by empowering you with emotional coping skills that will help you to not be overrun by fear. You can experience your feelings and let them inform you but not control you. This can foster a sense of self-mastery and also forge space for effective communication with others.

If you lean toward a secure attachment style, practicing mindfulness can help you become more aware of the present moment and train your brain to be able to shift from autopilot to mindful awareness. Stress reduction, improved mood, and a greater sense of well-being can support assertive communication goals and help you to maintain healthy relationships. Finally, these exercises can help individuals with an avoidant style connect to emotions that have been detached; they can become more aware of cues to guide assertiveness. If an avoidant attachment style describes you, mindfulness will teach you to focus on and notice your internal cues and validate your emotions.

One word of caution here: some women may need steps beyond these techniques to make sense of, process, and, in some cases, heal past wounds. Certain emotions and experiences, coupled with past personal and family histories and backgrounds, may require professional assistance to work through. If you've had trauma or chronic unresolved turmoil, know that a trained clinician can help you to tune in to and manage your experiences in a way that can help you find peace and closure.

There have been hundreds of emotional awareness exercises and management techniques developed through the years. I have found the six in this chapter to be among the most effective in my life and in the lives of my clients. I encourage you to familiarize yourself with them and practice them, as they will enable you to become attuned to your thoughts, feelings, wants, and needs—and prepare you to act assertively. ·

# CHAPTER 7

# Self-Expression: Doormat, Sword, and Lantern

In previous chapters, you've learned about your attachment style and history; the importance of tuning in to your thoughts, feelings, needs, and wants; and strategies to manage your emotions. Now we'll talk about three communication stances. We'll look at examples of each stance and how attachment style factors in.

Communication is assertiveness in action. How do you use your words, body language, tone, and other nonverbal cues to share your emotions, needs, and desires to others? My goal is to help you develop ways to approach others so your assertive communication will be more likely to be understood, heard, and respected. Expressing your feelings, thoughts, needs, and wants verbally is a key part of assertive communication, but it is only one component. Another aspect is your level of openness to the other person's point of view. It is in relationships that we develop into a person, and it is in relationships that we express our unique self. And how does your history and attachment style relate to all of this?

In my years of clinical practice, I have done *a lot* of coaching and role-playing with clients on how to approach delicate subjects in a way that is authentic, respectful, and, perhaps most of all, assertive. In order to combat the stereotype some individuals have of assertiveness (seeing it as synonymous with aggressiveness and pushiness), I wanted to come up with a way to represent assertiveness visually. As a songwriter, I often think in metaphors, and I drew upon my creativity to reframe this discussion. I now use the terms *doormat, sword*, and *lantern*. Though everyone uses each of the three at some point or another, I invite you to reflect on which communication stance you utilize most frequently.

# The Doormat

As its title suggests, an individual who assumes a doormat communication stance is often figuratively "run over" either by other people or simply by her own emotions. An individual who takes a Doormat stance doesn't want to disappoint anyone; though she likely genuinely cares about others, her people-pleasing behavior may actually be an attempt to feel validated, reassured, and loved. She may become easily frustrated and have a difficult time setting emotional boundaries. A woman with this stance may not be able to clearly identify and articulate her feelings, thoughts, needs, or wants; or she may choose to not assert them at all for fear of rejection, shame, or a threat to the relationship. She has learned to survive by "lying down" and allowing other people to make decisions for her.

A hidden payoff for the Doormat stance is the ability to blame others for negative things in your life, because they have the power and have made decisions you didn't make.

Have you ever felt like you should be the one continually sacrificing to make relationships work, as if that's your role? It could be a relationship in any setting—work, home, school—or type—friendly, professional, sexual, familial.

The Doormat stance of communication is often used when you're too overwhelmed by emotions (anxious attachment style), or because you're disconnected or cut off from your emotions (avoidant attachment style). Anxiously attached individuals will tend to overaccommodate in order to maintain the relationship; they may avoid rejection by making another person happy. Individuals with an avoidant style typically placate another person in order to not get too close to their own or to others' vulnerable emotions; they also tend to resign, give up, or care less. The Doormat stance lets *others* have it *their* way in order to avoid conflict and minimize experiencing uncomfortable emotions.

Years ago, I worked with a chronically ill woman in her thirties who had an anxious attachment style and often approached communicating in her relationships from the Doormat stance. In fact, I think Jane even said, "I'm sick and tired of being a doormat and getting walked over!" In trying to be a "good mother" and prevent her children from feeling neglected because of her health problems, she responded to their every request, regardless of whether it was realistic, healthy, or overly taxing to her physical or emotional health. For example, if one child didn't like what was being served for dinner, Jane would make an additional meal to placate the whining child. Although her intent was good, she was teaching them to treat her as someone whose sole existence was to meet their needs and keep them perpetually happy.

Through therapy, Jane and I worked to identify her feelings, thoughts, needs, and wants. She discovered that she was resentful toward her children and felt they were taking advantage of her willingness to do things for them without expressing any kind of appreciation. She learned to experience herself as a separate and valuable individual, distinct from her family, while still being able to maintain close relationships with them. This illustrates a move toward a higher level of differentiation. Through the process of differentiating herself from her family members, Jane was able to move from a Doormat stance toward a Lantern stance. Together we explored what she needed and wanted from them, and how to communicate assertively and set healthier boundaries.

Another client I worked with was a fifty-year-old male with an avoidant attachment style who often used the Doormat stance. Tim came into therapy because he desperately wanted to marry but was unable to maintain a long-term relationship with a woman. In past relationships, when things would start getting serious and his girlfriend wanted more commitment, he would break up with her in order to avoid conflict, pain, and feeling vulnerable. Tim had a habit of avoiding difficult conversations not only in his romantic relationships but in therapy sessions as well; he would often take the Doormat stance by agreeing with everything I said in what I assume was an attempt to be a likeable client. For example, in the first several sessions he didn't challenge anything I offered. He was agreeable to doing homework assignments and offered compliments about how I was the most helpful therapist he'd worked with.

As we continued our work together, it became clear that he used this strategy to protect himself and avoid feeling vulnerable to rejection. I encouraged Tim to feel free to speak up when he didn't agree with me in session and to also speak up more often in his relationships. This was a way for him to practice identifying and experiencing difficult emotions and expressing difference without severing his relationship (as he had done previously). Over time, Tim was able to maintain longer love relationships.

# The Sword

While the Doormat stance feels passive and weak, the Sword stance feels powerful—but only temporarily. Think about people who have drawn their swords and are ready for a fight. They are tense and willing to protect themselves at all costs. They want to keep you at a distance, and they may even want to hurt you. If you can relate to the sword stance, you may often feel irritable at seemingly trivial things. Underneath the sword you may sense that your self-worth is threatened and that you aren't emotionally safe. When disagreements arise, you may find yourself speaking and acting in ways that may be perceived as aggressive or hostile by others, even if that isn't your intent. Although the sword is there to protect your *primary* emotions (fear, sadness, vulnerability, loneliness), or the more vulnerable feelings underneath the irritability and anger that we talked about in chapter 5, it usually works against you because it pushes people away. It may help you protect yourself from feeling scared or sad or lonely and help you to feel safe, but it also creates disconnection with others.

The Sword stance also includes people who hide their sword so you can't see their weapon. This is also known as being passive-aggressive. I like to call it the *hidden* Sword stance. If this stance sounds familiar, you may find yourself trying to be "fine" or act calm, but when someone pushes you to the limit and you feel threatened, hurt, or vulnerable, you may pull out the sword. The sword may be concealed by a seemingly harmless Doormat stance, or it may be out of sight but at the ready behind your back. A common hidden Sword stance tactic is the use of biting humor that is then discounted by saying, "I was only joking. Can't you take a joke?" or "It's your fault you're hurt. Stop being so sensitive!"

Sarcasm can also be used as a hidden sword—you don't know when you're going to use your wit and humor in a way that comes across as biting or belittling (an approach that I find myself using more often than I'd like to admit). When you find yourself using a Sword stance it's likely because you're feeling scared and feel the need to protect yourself.

Similarly to individuals assuming a Doormat stance of communication, the Sword stance is more likely to be used if you have an insecure attachment style, either avoidant or "burned out" anxious attachment styles, and a lower level of differentiation. Because it's hard for individuals with these styles to distinguish between their thoughts and feelings (anxious attachment style) or to access their vulnerable emotions (avoidant attachment style), they tend to be emotionally reactive and have difficulty allowing space for another point of view. Sword stance is all about safety first—*emotional* safety, that is. If you feel fed up at being taken advantage of or not being heard (Doormat stance) it's easy to flip into an extreme response and lash out from a place of anger instead of out of a place of thoughtful response.

Using the sword as a primary stance is likely something you may have learned by being a recipient of criticism, harsh words, belittling comments, or even physical punishment or threat. If you regularly use the Sword stance in your relationships, you may want to reflect on how you learned to use the sword to protect yourself emotionally. Remember that the Sword stance is not about a desire to hurt others (although that happens), it's about a desire to *protect yourself* from being hurt again.

Having been a mother for twenty-five years, I have experienced the Sword stance a lot (and even used it a few times myself). At different points in their lives all four of my children have yelled, "I hate you, Mom!" or some similar angry sentiment. Sometimes it's been a toddler who doesn't want to go to bed. Other times it's a teenager who got caught breaking a family rule and doesn't want the consequences. The "I hate you, Mom!" statement is a classic example of a Sword stance tactic. Now, think about what a grown-up version of "I hate you!" may look like. The Sword stance in adults might be exhibited by disparaging a colleague during a work meeting. Or sharply accusing your friend of betraying a confidence before you get the whole story.

Remember in chapter 4 when we talked about the difference between primary and secondary emotions? The Sword stance is a great example of secondary emotions in action. There have been times when I have used the Sword stance in parenting situations. One incident I recall was a few years ago when my youngest daughter was around five years old. I had recently purchased a new Macbook Pro computer and was working on it while lying on the floor. Macy was upset about something and trying to get my attention, so she put her foot lightly on my new computer. I said, trying to be calm, "Macy, don't do that." She looked at me and did it again—she stepped on my brand new $1,500 computer! I can't recall what exactly I said or what I did but I do vividly remember being furious and responding to her very harshly (Sword stance).

My secondary emotion was fury, but underneath that, my primary emotion was fear—fear that she was going to break or damage my new computer—the place where I manage every part of my professional and personal life. I also think there was fear that I was a "bad mother" who can't control her child's behavior. What I felt first was fear, but that vulnerable emotion was quickly buried under anger about the fact that she defied me. The reason this situation is so fixed in my memory is because it was so rare. For most of my life I've used either the Doormat stance or the Lantern (which we'll talk more about in the next section). The Sword is the stance I use less frequently, but when I do, it's not pretty.

As I mentioned before, I myself learned a pattern of people-pleasing and caretaking, which led to being more accommodating (Doormat) than defensive (Sword). I have spent the better part of three decades learning how to communicate more effectively, through studying, practicing, doing therapy with hundreds of people, running a practice and managing employees, attending therapy myself, and maintaining a quarter century of marriage and family life. It's taken a long time to practice holding up the Lantern in difficult situations, but, over time, it has become a more natural response in many situations.

## The Lantern

I love lanterns. I collect handheld lanterns of all shapes and sizes. They all have handles and different colors of glass on the outside that protect the candle inside from being blown out. My therapy office and my home are decorated with lanterns. I love what they do—shed light and illuminate darkness.

The Lantern stance represents an assertive approach to communication and is the integration and application of all five skills of assertiveness: self-reflection, self-awareness, self-soothing, self-expression, and self-expansion. (We'll dive into the Lantern stance and its connection to self-expansion in the next chapter.)

When I am needing to practice what I preach about assertive communication, I imagine myself standing with my feet shoulder width apart, centered and balanced, holding up a lantern as high as I can reach and observing the situation. I envision myself standing up straight, feeling strong and not easily swayed. I imagine inviting the person I am interacting with to step into the lantern's light with me and ask this person to describe his or her experience and perspective. It allows for differing points of view to be seen and expressed. It is used to gain awareness of you and of the other person. *The Lantern stance is the goal for all attachment styles and for all assertive communication.*

If you have a secure attachment style and a higher differentiation level, the Lantern stance may come more naturally to you than to those with either anxious or avoidant styles. If you started this book with a secure style, you likely already have some degree of emotional awareness and are already able to distinguish your thoughts from your feelings. You are also probably more open to expressing differences of opinion while simultaneously holding space for another person's experience.

But if you have an insecure attachment style—more toward the anxious or the avoidant ends of the spectrum—you are probably more familiar with the Doormat or Sword stances. Take heart—you do not need to be a product of your past! You can still learn and practice strategies that will empower you to use a Lantern stance and act assertively. As you practice using the Lantern stance, your relationships will improve and your sense of efficacy and worth will grow.

## Soft Start-up

A helpful skill in developing a Lantern stance is approaching conversations with a "soft start." According to family researcher and psychologist John Gottman, how you *start* a conversation determines to a large degree how it will *end* (Gottman, Silver, and Nelson 1999). A *soft start-up* is the process of beginning a conversation with gratitude or a compliment and without criticism. It does not imply tiptoeing around the issue at hand; in fact, you begin by owning your perspective. It is about starting difficult conversations in a calm, mature, and respectful way that holds emotional space for differences. A soft start-up makes it more likely that the conversation will be productive and promote understanding and empathy. It also minimizes the chance of misunderstandings, which can lead to distance or disconnection. I have personally used, and have encouraged my clients to use, the soft start-up in conversations in many different settings—at work, school, church—and with friends, children, neighbors. Starting conversations with "I" instead of "you," and describing what *you* see and feel instead of blaming and criticizing, are examples of how to soften the start of a conversation.

A friend of mine was newly employed as a teacher at a treatment center for adolescent girls when she was called in by her boss to discuss some concerns reported by some of her students. The students had accused her of being unkind and unfair in the classroom and also of using inappropriate language. My friend's boss used a soft start by first asking how things were going for my friend in this new position, and then pointing out her strengths before bringing up a few key areas that needed improvement. The boss was also open to hearing her perspective by asking her if the accusations were true (instead of merely assuming that they were). My friend was able to share her side of the story, clarify some misconceptions (she'd never used inappropriate language), and also own some of the responsibility for things she needed to do better. Both women were able to end the conversation feeling valued and understood, and the classroom problem was resolved. It started and ended with softness and understanding.

## Cultivating Empathy

One of the most important features of the Lantern stance is the ability to feel and express empathy. Empathy in difficult conversations is tough and requires self-awareness and using the emotional management strategies we talked about in previous chapters (like mindfulness and wise mind). The ability to push the pause button on your own emotions enough to hold space to empathize with another person's point of view and emotions takes practice. To get a better understanding about what empathy *is*, I want to share Theresa Wiseman's four components of empathy (1996):

1. to be able to see the world as others see it

2. to be nonjudgmental

3. to understand another person's feelings

4. to communicate your understanding of that person's feelings

The last one is really important. Empathy is about communicating your understanding to the person you are talking to. It's not enough just to feel it inside of you. Empathy is a shared experience. These four aspects of empathy are crucial for developing a Lantern stance.

If you have a secure attachment style and a higher level of differentiation, it's likely that you will already know how to use the Lantern stance. You may be more aware of the times when you are taking a Doormat or Sword stance, which means you can consciously try to move back into Lantern stance.

It's important to remember that we use *all* of these communication stances at various times, and using one or the other doesn't make you a bad person. If one of the stances is your go-to mode of approaching conversations, it's likely how you learned to respond based on your relationship patterns, how you get your emotional needs met, and how you remain connected to your loved one. To be clear, this is *not* an excuse to use poor communication skills and to blame your family. Identifying your learned patterns is about developing understanding and awareness so you can make changes and become more effective in your assertive communication.

We talked about shame earlier, but I think it's worth revisiting here in relation to empathy. If you recall, researcher Brené Brown (2012) says that empathy is the only antidote to shame. When shame gets triggered by situations that threaten our ideal identity, or how we want to be perceived, it becomes particularly difficult to use the Lantern stance because we go into self-protection in order to hide our shame.

Here's a personal example of a time when I used empathy as an antidote to shame. My husband came to pick me up from the airport after, coincidentally, a week of training with Brené Brown. He had been working out of town a lot, so I appreciated the fact that he was home and willing to pick me up.

He asked me about my week. I started sharing some of the amazing aha moments that I'd had, and then I added, "But it was really tough to be all alone, with no one to celebrate with when I received such great news!"

He looked puzzled, and he asked very hesitantly, "Uh, now what great news are you talking about?"

Shocked, disappointed, puzzled, I looked at him and said sarcastically, "Oh, just that I was offered a *national book deal*, that's all."

"Oh, yes, that's right," he said sheepishly, and after a long pause asked, "Now…what was that book about again?"

I was crushed.

We had plunged into a shame spiral. My ideal of having an amazingly close marriage was threatened because I felt like my husband didn't seem to know (and care) about the details of my life. He was feeling shame because his ideal was on the line too. He wanted to think of himself as an attentive and caring husband, and this exchange seemed to highlight the disconnection we had both been experiencing but not wanting to admit.

I was faced with putting into practice what I had just spent the previous five days studying: how to experience vulnerability and respond empathetically, even when I am feeling intense emotion. So I continued talking.

"It took a lot of courage for you to ask me for clarification—I bet that was scary. Were you feeling shame?" I asked.

He replied, "Yes, it was scary to ask. But I should have remembered about your book contract. That *is* a big deal." It was actually the week I signed the contract with New Harbinger for *this* book! "You just have so many different projects going on that it's sometimes hard to keep things straight."

I replied, "I know. And you're working really hard right now, and we've both been under a tremendous amount of stress."

Acknowledging our shame, instead of hiding it, and practicing empathy—seeing it from my husband's perspective without judgment, trying to understand why he felt and acted the way he did, and to communicate my understanding—allowed us to maintain a Lantern stance instead of falling into a shame spiral.

Now that you're familiar with each of the three communication stances, let's explore which stance you use most often.

# AWARENESS EXERCISE
## What Is Your Go-To Stance?

Reflect on the following statements and see which one sounds and feels the most familiar to you. Remember that while you likely fall predominantly into one of these categories, each of us uses all three of the stances at different times.

### Doormat

When I'm upset I tend to stew about it rather than directly confront the situation.

When deciding on which restaurant to go to I rarely have strong preferences.

People know that if they bother me long enough, I'll give them what they want.

I tend to shut down when I'm feeling intense emotions.

I can move on quickly after being hurt.

### Sword

I make sure no one is going to take advantage of me.

If I think that a person is going to break up with me I break up first.

When I'm hurt, I tend to make snide remarks when others least expect it.

It is very important that people understand my point of view and agree with me.

I forgive but I never forget.

**Lantern**

There can be many different perspectives on the same situation.

When I'm upset, I can calm myself down quickly.

I rarely try to convince someone to agree with my point of view.

I am curious about another person's feelings, even if they're different from mine.

I can accept feedback, even when it's negative.

# Moving from Doormat or Sword to Lantern

If you are more familiar with Doormat or Sword stance, you may be thinking, "Oh, great! Now what? How do I move *toward* the Lantern stance so that it becomes my default stance?" It's all about practice. Practicing the skills outlined in previous chapters will move you toward the Lantern stance. Using the tools and ideas in the upcoming chapters will help you develop your Lantern stance. The final chapter of this book is dedicated entirely to incorporating the Lantern stance into your communication.

At this point you should know the difference between the Doormat, Sword, and Lantern stances, and be able to identify which is your go-to communication stance. Additionally, I hope you've gained a clear vision of what the Lantern stance looks like and feels like in conversations, and how it's related to your attachment style and differentiation level. In the following chapter you'll learn about the importance of boundaries and their relationship to attachment and differentiation. I'll outline a few of my most-used communication tools to help you become more assertive and to further develop your Lantern stance.

CHAPTER 8

# Self-Expression: Setting Strong Boundaries

In previous chapters, we've talked about how to identify your attachment style, your thoughts and emotions, and the three communication stances. In this chapter, we'll put all of this knowledge together to become a more effective communicator and move toward assertiveness. Throughout this book we've talked a lot about attachment, differentiation, and assertiveness—and how expressing your feelings, thoughts, needs, and wants is an expression of difference. In other words, asserting boundaries is part of defining a line that distinguishes you from others.

Sometimes the line we think we are drawing is too faint for others to see. All of us have shared thoughts and feelings with someone and been misunderstood, brushed aside, or worse, ignored. Can you think of a time when this happened to you? Maybe your word choice wasn't very smooth, your emotions were overwhelming, or you came off more intense than you intended. Maybe you weren't direct or clear enough. Maybe your body language wasn't congruent with your words. Or maybe your statements came at an inappropriate time or place. Whatever the reason, being rebuffed or rejected can be very discouraging.

I'm reminded of the TV show *The Office* in which, every episode, Michael Scott (played by Steve Carell) makes some type of insensitive, poorly timed, or rude comment in front of the entire office. From his ability to turn almost every conversation into a sexual innuendo ("That's what she said!") or to his constant berating of mild-mannered Toby in public ("Of all the idiots in all of the idiot villages in all of the idiot worlds, you stand alone."), it's clear that tact is not one of his strong points. I mean, who says that kind of stuff to coworkers?!

So let's get to some strategies that will help us *not* be like Michael Scott.

## Strategies for Starting a Difficult Conversation

Before you make assertive, courageous requests or statements, there are a few key things to keep in mind about how to best set the stage. Read on to learn how to create a situation in which it is most likely that your message, your intent, your mind, and your heart will be heard and respected by another person.

### Time It Right

In comedy, timing is everything. A great joke can fall flat if the comedian's timing is only slightly off. The same goes for assertive communication. Timing matters. A lot. It's a good idea to wait until your emotions are soothed enough for you to enter wise mind and identify and balance your emotions in a way that matches the message you're trying to convey.

Responding while experiencing an emotional flood is generally not the time to assert yourself. One exception would be in the case of physical self-protection, in the face of imminent danger to you or someone else. That is the reason we have the fight, flight, or freeze response! As we discussed in chapter 1, this survival response can help us run away from danger. However, most of the "danger" we face isn't physical danger—instead it's psychological and relational, and a quick emotional response may not be the best solution to the situation.

Here's an example of how better timing could have avoided a conflict. One day, a good friend had spoken to me in a very harsh and accusing tone (Sword stance). She was obviously upset, but I couldn't figure out what she was mad about. I expressed that I wanted her to slow down, that I was feeling worried that I had been misunderstood, and that I wanted a chance to clarify (Lantern stance). She was not in a place to hear my perspective, as she was preoccupied with her own. I ended the conversation and went home. Looking back, I can see that it would have been better to either hear her out or stop the conversation rather than trying to share my thoughts and feelings while she was obviously on emotional overload. In other words, it wasn't *my* time to be heard, it was hers. After a few days, I still felt hesitant to see her or speak with her. When I got up the courage, I asked if we could talk and if she was open to hearing my perspective and feelings (soft start). She was. When we met again—at a time when nerves were calmer—she apologized for her intensity and insensitivity in our previous conversation, and our connection was thankfully repaired.

## Seek Permission

In tempo with the "soft start" mentioned in chapter 6, it's important to approach the other person in a mild and open manner. Begin by inviting him or her into the conversation. Questions like, "Are you open to talking about what happened in the meeting this morning? When would be a good time?" or "I have a few thoughts and feelings I want to share with you about our conversation at lunch. Are you available now?" are clear cues to the other person that you want to talk to him or her, that the matter is important, and that you respect the person and want to talk when it's convenient for him or her. Asking permission to open a dialogue with "May I talk to you for a minute?" often gets better results than "We need to talk right now!"

## Keep It Private

When I was in elementary school it was common for teachers to correct students in front of classmates. I was generally a well-behaved child and got my work done, and I cringed when the teacher would give feedback or correction to a student in front of his or her peers. I knew how humiliating it would be if it were me receiving the criticism or correction.

In general, when you need to talk with someone and share your thoughts and feelings, particularly if it's an emotional topic, it's best to bring it up when there isn't an audience. This demonstrates maturity, is respectful and considerate to the other person, and creates a higher likelihood that your assertiveness will be well received and responded to. For example, if your mother-in-law is giving unsolicited parenting advice, instead of rolling your eyes and smirking in front of the extended family, hoping she gets the message, it would be better to pull her aside for a private chat and say, "I feel sad and mad when you suggest how I should parent my son because I think you don't trust me to be a good mother." It is much more likely that your assertive communication will be heard and valued if the person you're talking to isn't also having to manage feelings of humiliation or shame because other people are witnessing the conversation.

## Put Down Your Crystal Ball

We often get stuck in certain relationship patterns and repeat them over and over again. That's just what we do. And since relationships are circular and mutually created, it's easy to think that you can *always* predict how someone you know well will respond to your assertive communication based on your past interactions. My two youngest kids are masters at this; if they've had a disagreement or fight, they both will come to me hoping to align me with their point of view and "solve" their dilemma. When I direct them back to each other, they often say things like, "I've tried that before. She never listens to me!" or "He'll just say 'no I didn't' and slam the door in my face!" It's like they've already played out the conversation in their minds and are 100 percent certain of the outcome.

While we often do some sort of predicting the outcome of future conversations, we may inadvertently be *reinforcing* that particular outcome by our expectation (or certainty) that we already *know* the outcome. For example, if I go into a meeting with an employee who is going to be written up for failure to perform a particular aspect of his job, and I "know" that he will become defensive and start blaming and belittling me, then I may unknowingly present the feedback to him in a way that makes it *more likely* that he will actually behave in the way I assumed he would respond. And the truth is that we all like to be right about our predictions of others; it makes us feel in control. But too often, in expecting and preparing for the worst, we actually foster an outcome that we don't want.

I'm not saying don't rehearse conversations in your mind; it's a good idea to mentally and emotionally prepare for any outcome or reaction. I am saying that rehearsing conversations in your mind and envisioning the other person hearing you and validating you makes it more likely that your communication will be clearly received by the other person. It's the concept of a self-fulfilling prophecy. We want to be right, so we act in ways that make our predictions or beliefs about other people come true.

Also, *listen* to what the other person has to say. She may have some valuable feedback. Give her a chance to express things from her perspective. Communication always goes both ways. Remember how the fifth component of assertiveness, self-expansion, is a sensitivity to the other person's experience? This comes into play here.

## Breathe, Just Breathe

If you're feeling intense, overwhelming emotions, it's probably best to wait a while until you assert yourself. As we've talked about previously in this book, when your survival brain kicks in, you go into fight, flight, or freeze mode and temporarily disconnect from the prefrontal cortex, or the conscious, problem-solving part of your brain. Pausing to take a slow breath—even just one breath—can take your nervous system down a few notches so you can reconnect with the conscious, intentional part of your brain and respond to the situation in ways that will help instead of hurt you and your relationships.

## Push the Pause Button

An emotional skill that is helpful to develop (and these are all skills that you need to practice in order to develop and master over time) is what I call "push the pause button." It's like those times when you're enjoying your favorite television show and you look down at your cell phone to see that your sibling is calling. You're really into your show, and you know that your father's health hasn't been good lately. So, what do you do? You push the pause button on your show and answer your phone. The TV show hasn't gone away. It's just stopped temporarily while you attend to something more pressing. It is the same with our emotions. If our emotions are like the show, developing and moving across the screen, we can learn to pause them—not numb, deny, or bury them—so we can come back to them later.

This skill comes in handy not only in intimate relationships but also in professional settings, where you likely have to keep your cool in stressful situations. For example, if someone interrupts you during a work meeting, it may remind you of how your older sister used to talk over you at the dinner table while you were sharing something exciting about your day. A flood of past negative experiences compounded by the immediate emotional event might feel overwhelming to you, so it would probably be best to push the emotional pause button, take a moment to identify your feelings (mindfulness), reflect on why your response is so intense, and wait to do more work on this at a later time.

## Strategies for Getting Your Message Across

Some of the above techniques may come naturally to you or seem quite obvious, but others may not be as familiar to you or require greater effort on your part. They are all about being tactful, discreet, sensitive, and wise to help create an optimal opportunity for your own assertiveness. You won't master them all at once. I suggest starting with the technique that you feel most confident about putting into practice right now. Practice that specific technique for one or two weeks until it feels even more comfortable. Then select another skill to focus on for a couple of weeks.

So with the stage set for positive communication to take place, what else can you do to get your message across? Let's explore this more.

## Use More Than Words

Now I want you to hone in on one specific aspect of family relationships that applies directly to assertiveness: communication. Communication refers to sending and receiving messages with other individuals. While communication is one way that we can convey love and affection, it's also a powerful method of expressing the inherent differences that naturally arise in relationships. In other words, communication is a way to connect *with* others, as well as a way to differentiate yourself *from* others.

When two people are together, there is always communication happening, messages being sent about yourself and the other person. But communication is more than the words you say—it is *how* you say them. Your tone of voice, body language, level of eye contact, raise of an eyebrow, exasperated sigh, and more are all part of communication. An often-overlooked aspect of communication is the power of what is *not* spoken. You might think that *not* responding to someone is the same as not communicating. Lack of response is still communication. "*One cannot not communicate*: Every behavior is a form of communication" (Watzlawick, Beavin, and Jackson 1967, 51).

A recent personal experience confirmed the power of non-verbal cues in relationships. My thirteen-year-old son is very sensitive to my breathing. I know that may sound strange, but it's true. When my breathing changes, like when I sigh unconsciously, he will sometimes check in with me, sweetly asking, "Are you okay, Mom? You sound tired." Sometimes it's startling (and even slightly troubling) to realize that I am communicating strong messages even when I don't know it! You cannot *not* communicate.

Since we are always communicating something about ourselves or about others, my goal in writing this book is to help you become more conscious of your inner life and to develop the skills to accurately and powerfully express your feelings, thoughts, needs, and wants through words *and* through action, instead of communicating from a place of habitual repetition or emotional wounding from the past.

A place to start for tuning in to your nonverbal communication is to notice your tone of voice and your body language in a conversation. For example, imagine you're telling a friend how much fun you had on vacation last week, but your voice sounds monotone and has no joy in it—your words and your voice are sending incongruent messages. If you're responding to feedback from a manager about your job performance and you say, "Thank you for the feedback. I'll take it into consideration and make those changes," imagine that while you're saying those words your body is turned away and your arms are crossed—you're sending a message through your body that undermines your words.

So, in an upcoming conversation, take note of the messages your body is sending compared to your verbal expression. Then reflect on the following questions:

Does my tone of voice reinforce or reverse what I am trying to convey verbally? Is my body language supporting what I am saying or is it sending a mixed message?

## Build a Strong Fence

Central to the conversation of assertiveness is the concept of boundaries. Boundaries are like the membrane of a cell. The membrane differentiates the cell as a self-contained unit and also mediates what comes into the cell and what is expelled. Similarly, boundaries are what enable us to define ourselves as unique individuals while simultaneously allowing us to interact with others. Where and how we set our boundaries moderates our balance between being a distinct individual and being interconnected with others. Boundaries can be physical, like our comfort level with how close a person is standing to us on a bus, or they can be abstract, like when an acquaintance asks an intrusive question, such as "Why aren't you married, yet?" or "When are you going to have kids?"

When I teach clients about boundaries I often use a fence metaphor. If your boundaries are weak, they're like a fence without strong posts that can be easily pushed over. This is a common pattern in women with an anxious attachment style and a low level of differentiation. To see how this might play out in real life, let's look at what happened to a single friend of mine, Gina, who has an anxious attachment style. She had complained that a coworker kept asking her out. She had no interest in dating him, but instead of communicating that directly she agreed to go out with him occasionally. Other times she made up excuses for why she couldn't go out with him. Gina didn't want to hurt his feelings and feared he might talk poorly about her to coworkers. This led to Gina being more anxious at work because she was trying to avoid her coworker. When he finally found out that she had no interest in him he was angry and hurt. By not establishing her boundaries, Gina created the very result that she feared—she deeply hurt his feelings and he spoke negatively about her to others for several months afterward.

On the other hand, if your boundaries are too rigid, it's as if you've built a high stone wall with no gate to enter or exit: nothing comes in or goes out. While your fortress wall will keep you safe, it will also prevent you from being known and from knowing others. It will stifle your ability to develop intimate relationships.

If your attachment style leans toward the avoidant with a low level of differentiation, you may be more familiar with the stone wall approach to boundaries than the unstable fence. Although it may seem that thick, rigid boundaries would indicate a high level of differentiation, that's not the case. Highly differentiated people with a secure attachment style are able to build a strong fence with an inviting gateway that they can open or shut, and not a stone wall. Individuals with a high differentiation level are able to be separate from (fence) *and* connected to others (gate), and can effectively filter what comes into their emotional space, and what and how much they share with others.

One of the most important things to understand about boundaries is that *you* are the one who creates them. Whether you're aware of this or not, you decide what kind of a fence you'll build and what comes in and out of your personal space— physical and emotional. Every person has the right and responsibility to be able to say when someone else is too close, too dependent, or too involved or intertwined (this is where assertiveness comes in). You choose your company. If you are not comfortable with someone or something, you are allowed to express that. And perhaps the most fundamental boundary is the right to say no. Saying no is the primary way we express "I am me. I am not you. We are different."

## Practice Saying No

As a mother of four, I am acutely aware that one of the first things children learn to say is the word "no." I've heard it from the shrill cries of a two-year-old lying on the floor refusing to go to bed and from the sarcastic voice of a teen who doesn't want to turn off the video game. Although it's usually not a word that parents want to hear in response to their requests, it's one of the most important words for a child to learn. The ability to say no is a first step in communicating the awareness of difference. I am me. I am *not* you. I think, feel, want, and need different things.

While the ability to express difference is developmentally crucial for a child's development of a sense of self, many women lose their no as they get older. For young women raised in Western culture, this shift often happens during adolescence— the silencing of thoughts, feelings, wants, and needs in exchange for the love and approval of others. Author and psychologist Mary Pipher beautifully describes this tragic process in her book *Reviving Ophelia: Saving the Selves of Adolescent Girls* (1994):

> As a girl, Ophelia is happy and free, but with
> adolescence she loses herself. When she falls in love
> with Hamlet, she lives only for his approval. She has no
> inner direction; rather she struggles to meet the
> demands of Hamlet and her father. Her value is
> determined utterly by their approval. Ophelia is torn
> apart by her efforts to please. When Hamlet spurns her
> because she is an obedient daughter, she goes mad with
> grief. Dressed in elegant clothes that weigh her down,
> she drowns in a stream filled with flowers." (4)

While the fact that you are reading this book proves that your life hasn't literally ended tragically like the character of Ophelia, you may have figuratively killed parts of yourself in order to gain love and approval from others, or to avoid rejection or disconnection in relationships. I know I did. Women often "kill" their willingness to say the word no.

I recall being around eleven or twelve when I started silencing my voice and losing my no. I would answer most questions with "I don't know." I remember one of my mom's friends asking me a question, and when I replied, "I don't know," she called me out. She said, "If you don't know what you want, who will? If you don't decide I'll assume it's a no." Thirty-five years later I still remember the impact of her noticing that I was starting to silence my "voice" in my own life.

## Why It's Hard to Say No

In my clinical work with women, and after a decade of doing self-care workshops, these themes have emerged as common barriers to saying no. See if any of them sound familiar:

- I don't want to disappoint others.

- I should be able to do it all.

- I'm afraid to say no because people will think less of me.

- I want to help.

- If I say no, I'll feel guilty.

- I want to please others.

- I feel pressured by others.

- If I say no, people will stop asking me.

- If people ask me, it must be important to them.

- If I don't do it, no one else will.

- If I can't do it all, it means I am weak, unwilling, or not good enough.

- I don't want to add to another person's burden.

- I don't want other people to say no to me when I ask them for something.

- I feel that I owe it to some people to always say yes because they have done so much for me.

- I want to be generous and giving, and saying no feels selfish (Hanks 2013).

As we talked about in chapter 2, women are generally socialized from very early on to be caretakers and to be sensitive to the needs and feelings of others. Sometimes this aspect of socialization impacts women's ability to set boundaries and to say no. To be clear, I am not saying that sensitivity to our interconnectedness is a negative thing. In my own life it has been both a blessing and a challenge—a double-edged sword. I have often taken on emotional burdens that are not mine, but it has also allowed me to quickly connect with clients and to empathize deeply. However, the awareness of others' needs should be balanced with self-awareness and permission to express your unique self.

Moving from an individual perspective to a cultural perspective, it is important to note that, historically, women have learned to please others as a way to access some degree of power in order to get their own needs met. For example, a century ago, when women didn't have access to many professions or high-paying jobs, they may have learned to keep their husband happy in order to have freer access to "his" money. Those who have less power please those in power, often in order to survive. In addition to individual and family socialization based on gender, we have inherited the patterns of thousands of years of women needing to silence their voices due to oppression and gender inequality. A part of that heritage is the fear of saying no, especially to those who are in positions of power.

## AWARENESS EXERCISE
## Exploring the Meaning of No

Consider the following statements or questions to understand why it might be challenging for you to say no.

- In what situations do I have difficulty saying no when I know I should?

- If I say no, I'm afraid that...

- If I say no, it means that...

- What messages did I hear or learn from my early experiences about saying no?

- How did my parents respond when I said no to them as a child or teen?

- How do I feel when I say yes when I really want to say no?

For a worksheet version of this exercise, visit **http://www.newharbinger.com/33377**.

Giving yourself permission to say no and prioritizing your needs as equal to others may contradict what you learned in your early relationships. The idealized image of women as willing to sacrifice themselves at all costs for the sake of others is potent. Ironically, learning how to set healthy boundaries and to be assertive allows you to be *more* effective in caring for and in meeting the needs of others. The more differentiated you are and the more you move toward a secure attachment style, the more available you can be to other people.

## Why No Is Important

Over the years, I've learned that people often aren't as fragile as we think they are, yet we try to protect them from hurt feelings by saying yes when we mean no. I regularly remind myself that no one ever died from being disappointed. Being able to say no has been a really important skill for me in keeping my priorities straight and sparing myself the guilty feelings that come from failing to do or be everything that everyone else wants (or what I *think* everyone else wants). For example, I've gotten good at graciously saying no to speaking and singing invitations unless it sounds fun and energizing and works with my family's schedule. It's liberating to know that giving an honest no allows me to focus on what really matters most in my life.

In addition to no being a fundamental boundary and part of the differentiation process, there are other compelling reasons to give yourself permission to say no. Using no means that you accept that you are a human being and have limitations. As much as we want to be all and do all and keep everyone happy, we can't! We have a certain number of hours in the day and a certain threshold where stress becomes toxic. No also prevents burnout by filtering out things that we can't or don't want to do, keeping us from being overwhelmed and overcommitted. It allows us to focus on the things that matter most.

## Finding the Words to Say No

I've found that having certain go-to phrases for turning down an invitation or a request makes it easier for me—and for other women—to say no. As an emotional health contributor on a local women's lifestyle TV show, I have done a few interviews on how to say no and set healthy boundaries. When I do TV appearances I will often create graphics to go along with the main points in the interview. One of the most shared graphics is one that offers the following helpful phrases for saying no:

"That's just not going to work for me."

"I can't give you an answer right now, will you check back with me?"

"I want to, but I'm unable to."

"I'm not able to commit to that right now."

"I really appreciate you asking me, but I can't do it."

"I understand you really need my help, but I'm just not able to say yes to that."

"I'm going to say no for now. I'll let you know if something changes."

"I'm honored that you would ask me, but my answer is no."

"No, I can't do that, but here's what I *can* do…"

"I just don't have that to give right now" (Hanks 2013).

Now you know the importance of reclaiming and using your no as a fundamental boundary and a fundamental expression of differentiation. You're also now prepared with specific phrases to help you say no. So let's explore the topic of boundaries further. There is a lot more to boundaries than saying no.

## Receive the Gift of Resentment

How do you know that you need to assert yourself by setting a boundary, clarifying a boundary, or setting a firmer boundary? What are the physical, behavioral, or emotional signs you need to assert yourself? While there can be many signals that your boundaries are being crossed, I have found one emotion in particular is a consistent indicator to me that I need to take some sort of action relating to boundaries. That emotion is resentment. I call it "the gift of resentment."

Resentment is an angry feeling that you experience when you think you've been treated unfairly or when a situation has garnered an unfair result. Resentment has helped me to set boundaries regarding certain aspects of my professional life. Several years ago, I realized that I was starting to resent seeing clients in the afternoon because my children were home and I wanted to be home with them. My feelings of resentment helped me to muster up the courage to change my work hours and to assertively "hold the lantern" when telling my clients about my decision.

If you feel resentment toward a person or a situation, it's worth examining the trigger closer. If you find yourself obsessing over a comment a friend made last week to the point where it interferes with your peace of mind, you may need to address it directly and assertively. If you find yourself feeling resentment picking up after your children, you may need to clearly define your expectations. Maybe you sense that a friendship is one-sided because it seems you're the one most often initiating getting together. If you are experiencing feelings of resentment or lingering discomfort, these are signs that you need to make some kind of change, assert yourself, or set a boundary in a relationship.

I'm reminded of a conversation I had with a caller during my brief stint hosting a call-in radio show. Helen had several young children, and her seventy-year-old mother lived just down the street. Because she loved and cared for her mother, who struggled with bouts of depression and was lonely after losing her husband, Helen wanted to include her in their family's life. But Helen began to feel overly burdened. Our conversation about boundaries went something like this:

*Helen:* I never grew up with my grandparents, so I'm grateful my kids have time with their grandma. But sometimes she crosses a line and gets involved in trying to parent my children. I feel guilty when I go shopping by myself with my baby because we live in a small town thirty minutes from the nearest shopping area, and I feel like I should invite her to come. I don't like feeling guilty and resentful. I know she is lonely, but she doesn't do a whole lot to increase her circle of friends.

*Julie:* Who is responsible for her loneliness?

*Helen:* I know, she is...But I feel bad because my mom doesn't have my dad. And he was her life. [Her voice started quivering.] I don't know how to fill that void for her. I was so focused on her loss after my dad died that I realized, eight years later, that I haven't grieved *my* loss. My dad won't ever know my kids.

*Julie:* So, this pattern of taking on your mother's pain and trying to make it better is nothing new. It's been going on for a long time?

*Helen:* Yes, I was raised on guilt. It's so hard to break guilt.

*Julie:* Who is responsible for your mom's loneliness? Her loneliness is *her* responsibility. You've tried for years and you haven't been able to take it away. Your main stewardship is your little family; they need to come first. You can't bring your dad back, and your mom doesn't seem to want to create another life without him. The better you get at letting go of carrying *her* pain, the more energy you'll have to love and support her.

*Helen:* It's hard to let go of…and lately it's getting more difficult to be around her because she tends to be very negative.

*Julie:* Maybe it's time to give her some feedback about her negativity. You can set boundaries by simply saying, "I really can't hear this right now, I've got to go." You can do it in a respectful, loving way. It's time to protect your emotional resources and stay in *your* business. You're at risk for getting stress-related illness caring for five kids, working an extra job, volunteering at church, and caring for an aging parent.

*Helen:* I want to give the best of me to my five children. I don't want to be spent and exhausted all of the time. I know this is awful, but I've thought that when she dies I'll miss her and also be pretty relieved. And then I feel even more guilty.

*Julie:* It's "the gift of resentment" telling you that you need to set a boundary or do something differently. Change the way you're interacting with her. You're in charge of what you take on and what you don't. You are responsible to honor her, and help her, but you're not responsible *for* her happiness. If you can let go of that expectation for yourself, you'll find you can enjoy her more. So your question is really, "How do I love and support someone without taking on her emotions?" Setting stronger boundaries will not only help you get rid of your resentment but it may also help your kids feel less resentful toward their grandma for taking time and energy away from them. Have you thought about ways you could ask her to support you, so the relationship could feel more mutual? Does she ever tend your children? If she is so bored and lonely, let her help you, too.

*Helen:*  Oh, I needed to hear that. Thank you so much for taking my call.

In this conversation, Helen was conflicted about changing the boundaries with her mother because she felt obligated to do everything she could to support her. However, her ongoing resentment was her clue that she needed to rethink her boundaries. Helen needed to modify them in a way that addressed her resentment while still allowing her to see herself as an attentive and nurturing daughter—part of her ideal identity. This is also an example of differentiation in her relationship with her mother. The resentment Helen felt about doing so much for her mother was complicated by feelings of guilt because she was viewing setting boundaries as being equivalent to abandonment. In trying to be a loving daughter, Helen created more stress for herself and enabled her mother to not take responsibility for her social needs and to not cultivate other relationships. And in doing this Helen was inadvertently crossing her mother's emotional boundaries.

## Stand Your Ground

Having strong boundaries requires you to mean what you say and stand your ground. Sometimes women have a tendency to apologize for things that don't warrant an apology. Have you ever said anything potentially assertive and/or uncomfortable by starting with, "Hey, sorry to bother you, but…" or "Sorry, hope this isn't weird…"? I think one of the main reasons we unnecessarily apologize is because we are afraid of coming off as intimidating or intrusive. But keep in mind that *your* voice deserves to be heard and valued just as much as the next person's. Incessant apologizing may undermine your message or weaken your boundary. Save your sorries for when you've truly done something wrong, not for when you make valid assertions by sharing your feelings, thoughts, wants, and needs, or expressing difference.

One further way you can stand your ground is by bringing your body language into alignment with your words. Much of our communication is nonverbal. If our verbal communication and our body language aren't in harmony, most people will give more weight to your body than your words. Tried-and-true strategies, like maintaining eye contact and not slumping or slouching over, can indicate that what you're saying is important. Resist any urge to "hide" or distract yourself to lessen the directness of the exchange; no playing with your iPhone when being assertive! Thinking back to the stances of communication, someone with a Doormat stance may struggle with the ability to exhibit confidence in her body language, while a person with a Sword stance may appear dominating or confrontational. The key again is to seek the Lantern stance: self-respecting enough to carry yourself in a way that matches your words. And if by chance you're still nervous or even scared to assert yourself? All you can do is your best. I love the saying by activist Maggie Kuhn: "speak your mind, even if your voice shakes" (Kuhn, Long, and Quinn 1991, 159). As we will continue to discuss, all these skills require practice, so be patient with yourself as you are learning them and applying them.

## Respect Others' Boundaries

While establishing and communicating your boundaries is important, it's only one side of the story. The other part of healthy assertive communication is being aware and respectful of someone *else's* boundaries. And even though it may not be pleasant to accept, the truth is that you yourself have probably crossed a fence or two before. Have you ever been clingy? Asked or expected too much of another person? Taken on responsibility for "fixing" a loved one's problem? I know I have!

Unfortunately, sometimes we make the mistake of not being sensitive to the feelings, energy, and time of others. And the signs that you've overstepped your bounds are usually the same as when someone has done the same to you: the other person avoids you, resents you, seems frustrated and exhausted, and the relationship seems to be strained.

Your crossing of someone's boundary may be well intentioned. Maybe you want to help someone you love or "fix" his or her problem, like Helen wanted to fix her mother's loneliness. But doing so not only unnecessarily burdens you, it also communicates that you don't trust the other person to handle his or her life. I love the words of author Byron Katie, who says that there are only three kinds of businesses in this world: your business, other people's business, and "God's business" (Katie and Mitchell 2002). "God's business" here means anything that is *not* under your control and *not* under other people's control, like earthquakes or the untimely death of a loved one. An example of getting into other people's business would be thinking or saying, "You need to take better care of your health" or "You really need to spend more time with your children while they're still young."

You may be thinking, "Wait! What's wrong with being concerned about someone else's well-being and making helpful suggestions for how they can improve their lives?" According to Katie, when you venture into other people's business or "God's business," you create stress and pain for yourself. Additionally, when you get out of your own business you create disconnection from yourself (the opposite of mindfulness) and disconnection from others. How can you be connected to yourself if you are not *in* your own life? How can you be connected to others in a healthy way if you aren't in your own life? Being in other people's business or "God's business" is indicative of a lower level of differentiation of self—not being clear where you end and where someone else begins. Strong boundaries means *staying in your own business!*

How does all of this relate to taking the Lantern stance in our communication? First, acknowledging and honoring *your* boundaries should naturally lead you to doing the same for another person. Also, when you find that you've stepped on someone's toes, it takes confidence, humility, and certainly assertiveness to say something like, "Did I hurt you when I did that?" or "I apologize if I didn't respect your boundary in that situation." Being willing to admit your own wrongdoings and owning your mistakes is a sign of emotional maturity that will strengthen and sustain your relationships.

There are many reasons why we don't respect someone else's boundaries. We might've been raised with very different boundary expectations in our early relationships. For example, families vary in how they use physical touch. Some families hug, kiss, and sit next to each other, while other families only shake hands and pat shoulders. If you're from a touchy family, it would be easy to overstep the boundary of a friend or colleague who was raised in a family culture that showed affection in ways other than physical touch.

Pay attention to nonverbal cues—they often speak louder than words, as mentioned earlier in this chapter. Watch for closed body language: turning away, folding arms and legs, walking backward. Also, notice when someone pulls away by not responding to your text, e-mails, or phone calls; they may be trying to send you a different kind of message.

While it's important to be sensitive to others' verbal and nonverbal communication regarding *their* boundaries, it is your responsibility to make your boundaries very clear. Now that you've learned strategies to help you understand your emotional cues, and you've been given the skills to initiate conversations and set boundaries, let's learn about tools for assertive communication. They're really simple. And I can't wait to share them with you!

## Formula for Assertive Communication

During my undergraduate studies, I took a communication course as part of my general education credits. I don't remember the name of the course, who taught it, or what books we read— it was more than twenty-five years ago. The only thing I remember is this simple sentence for assertive communication:

I feel _____ when you _____ because I think _____.

This template is one of my favorite tools. It simplifies assertive expression by making it easier to share feelings and thoughts in a way that is more likely to be heard and understood by another. I actually use this tool in my own relationships all the time. For example, I just said to one of my adult children at dinner, "I feel mad when you text during dinner because I think that my requests aren't important to you." Or to my friend and colleague, Clair, "I feel excited that you got your article published because I think you are one of the most gifted therapists I know!" It is a simple way to separate my thought and my feeling, as well as give specific feedback about what I am emotionally responding to. As you may recall, differentiation is knowing the difference between your thoughts and feelings, and managing the ebb and flow of separateness and connection with others. I hope you find this tool helpful, too. Let's explore how it might work for you.

## AWARENESS EXERCISE
## What's Bothering You?

Think of a relationship situation that is bothering you right now. Maybe your coworker has been complaining to you about the poor quality of work coming from another coworker. You don't like how you feel—you think it's none of your business—and you want to ask her to stop, but you're afraid that she'll be offended. Or maybe your spouse seems to ignore you when you try to talk about finances, or your adult child is living at home and not pulling his or her weight in contributing to the household.

Now try articulating your concern more clearly by formatting it to fit into this sentence. "I feel _____ [your emotion] when you _____ [another's specific behavior] because I think _____ [the thought you have about it]."

Here are a few examples:

- I feel sad when you come home from work and turn on the TV because I think I'm not important to you.

- I feel hurt when you leave my name off of a presentation we worked on together because I think you don't value my contribution to the team.

- I feel mad when you leave your backpack and jacket on the floor because I think you don't care about your belongings.

- I feel sad when you don't include me in Girls' Night Out because I think I'm not important to you.

You can use this sentence format to effectively share any kind of emotion or thought in your relationships. Think about using this formula for assertive communication while using the Lantern stance: standing on your own two feet, holding up a lantern, illuminating and observing the situation with openness to hearing and validating the other person's experience.

Try visualizing yourself expressing what's bothering you assertively, starting with the "I feel _____ …" statement using the Lantern stance. Particularly when describing the other person's behavior (the "because you _____"), it's important to be very specific. For example, "I felt afraid when you asked me to work overtime last week because I thought you were questioning my productivity and time management during work hours" is more helpful than "I don't like it when you ask me to work so much because I think you think I'm a slacker." The second statement is less specific and therefore a lot less clear. The phrase "asked me to work overtime last week" is a lot more specific than "ask me to work so much," and "questioning my productivity and time management" is a lot more specific than "you think I'm a slacker."

This communication formula we're discussing isn't just about sharing painful or difficult feelings. It can also help you better articulate positive expressions: "I feel happy when you touch my hand because I think you care about me. Thanks for doing that." Specific feedback, whether negative or positive, is always clearer and more meaningful to the receiver. More often than not, open, direct, and honest communication will help you share your experience *and* make direct requests of others. It will also help others understand you.

## How to Make Assertive Requests

To clarify, the purpose of being assertive, speaking up, and making requests is not so you will get everything you want or get other people to change. Sometimes people will respond favorably to your assertiveness, and sometimes they won't. Either way, it's still worth expressing. If you'll recall in chapter 5, we talked about the importance of healthy emotional expression and the importance of getting the *e-motion* out of you so it doesn't fester. Whether or not you get what you want after you express yourself, you will be contributing to your emotional health and reaffirming your sense of self.

Making direct requests of others doesn't mean acting demanding or stern. For example, here is another one of my go-to phrases that I use when I am holding a Lantern stance: "It would mean a lot to me if…" The reason this phrase is so effective is because it starts with owning that this request is *you* wanting it—that it is meaningful to *you*. It allows you to hold space for the possibility that it won't be important to the person with whom you're communicating. This makes it more likely that the other person will remain open to hearing your request and won't shut down or become defensive. To illustrate, here are some ways of making requests that tend to put people on the defensive:

*Why don't you ever...*

*What would it take to get you to...*

*You should...*

*If you really cared about me, you would...*

*I wish you would do _____ without me having to ask!*

*Don't you think you should...?*

What are, if any, emotional responses to these phrases? Are any of them familiar to you either because you've used them or because they've been used by others? Now compare the above phrases to the following request sentence stems:

*It would mean a lot to me if...*

*I would appreciate it if you would...*

*I'd like it if you would...*

*I loved it when you did _____. Will you do that again?*

Can you see the difference between the first group of phrases and the second? The first group of phrases feels icky, manipulative, blaming, or guilt-trippy. The second group feels straightforward, clear, and confident. My goal is to help you create situations where it is more likely for you to be heard and understood, and where you can hear and understand another person.

## OSCAR: Assertiveness in Action

Now that you know the definition and importance of setting boundaries, why and how to say no, how resentment signals the need to look closer at your boundaries, an assertive communication formula, and a phrase for making requests of others, we're going to tie it all together by using my assertive communication map mnemonic OSCAR. Be sure to take a Lantern stance when using this tool.

*Observe the situation.* Notice what is happening without judgment (remember this from mindfulness practice?). It's helpful to stick to the facts and not your beliefs about the situation. For example, an observing thought might be, "She just told the boss, in front of me, that she put the presentation together all by herself. I helped her with it last week." A judging or evaluating response might be, "She's such a backstabber! Always trying to kiss up to the boss and make herself look better than everyone else." Do you see the difference? The first statement is based on an observation of the facts of the situation, and the second is based on an interpretation of the facts.

*Sort thoughts and feelings.* After you've observed the situation, reflect on your response. Identify your thoughts and your feelings. Pausing for a moment to reflect helps create a healthy distance between you and your response so you don't overidentify (often experienced by those with an anxious attachment style) with your thoughts and feelings, or you don't underidentify (common with an avoidant attachment style). This is related to the wise mind exercise in chapter 6 where you identified your emotional mind and your rational mind; this practice is also a part of differentiation of self.

*Compassionately communicate.* Once you've observed the facts, identified your response, and have successfully balanced your emotions, it's time to put your assertive communication skills into practice. Using the Lantern stance, along with the formula "I feel _____ when you _____ because I think _____" helps you to own your experience while simultaneously holding space for the other person's experience.

This is part of developing a higher level of differentiation: you are clear about your experience so you can accept another person's experience, even if it's drastically different. Compassionate communication allows you to be you—to be separate—and still remain connected and open to the other person.

*Ask questions.* Now that you have a good handle on your own experience and have clearly conveyed it, the next step is to invite the other person to share his or her experience—in other words, to invite them into the light of your Lantern. Questions like, "How do you see things?" or "What's going on for you right now?" allow the other person to express his or her experience, even if it's different, in the safe emotional space you're holding open for him or her. This is also an opportunity to demonstrate empathy in your responses to what is shared.

*Request directly and clearly.* Once the other person feels heard and understood, make your request. For example, if you want someone to do something differently, here's your chance to use the phrase "It would mean a lot to me if..." (Note that this is also an example of the soft start-up mentioned in chapter 6.) Remember that this is not a *demand*, it's a *request*, and the other person may or may not respond to your request in the way that you hope. If the other person doesn't, then you can go through this process again, observing what's happening in the moment, and continuing through the OSCAR steps.

Being *specific* is incredibly important in making requests in assertive communication. For example, consider Sara, an adult who is uncomfortable with her parents frequently giving her children expensive and extravagant gifts. While Sara is grateful for their love and willingness to please their grandchildren, the gifts have become excessive and are more than she feels are appropriate for them to have. She realizes she needs to set a boundary and communicate with her mother and father. Pulling them aside privately, Sara can say, "We are so grateful for the gifts you give our kids; they are very thoughtful, and the kids love them! But we're trying to teach them to enjoy material possessions in moderation, and the gifts are becoming a bit much. We feel it's best if you limit the gifts to one per child every three months. How would you feel about that?"

Sara properly set the stage by ensuring privacy and then being very clear about the boundary she expected. Saying something like, "We need you to cut back on the gift-giving" might have been too vague and left her parents unsure about what she needs. But by being specific about how many and how often, she paved the way for her request to be responded to in a positive way.

Another point this example illustrates is the importance of possibly providing a context, or reasoning, for your request. Sara gave her mother and father a legitimate reason for her appeal; she wanted to be judicious in how often her kids played with fancy toys. If you can clearly communicate your *why* so that the other person can understand where you're coming from, he or she will hopefully be more receptive to what you have to say. I would advise, however, that you don't let your descriptions get too lengthy:

"I don't want the kids to become too materialistic, and we already got a new iPad for Christmas. Plus, their gadgets can occupy so much of their time that they don't spend time with their friends. And I'm also afraid that spoiling them will make them selfish and feel like they're entitled."

This kind of explanation may be unnecessarily long. Elaborate enough, but strive for brevity too. Each situation is unique—what is appropriate should be determined on a case-by-case basis. The steps of OSCAR—available in handout form at **http://www.newharbinger.com/33377**—are a great general guide when practicing assertive expression.

## OSCAR Examples

Interestingly, while working on a draft of this very chapter, I met with my writing assistant over lunch at a local restaurant. As we talked through the chapter outline, she was frequently checking her phone and responding to texts. As our conversation continued, her texting became more and more distracting to me. I felt torn. We were working and I was paying her for her time, so I was bugged. *And* I also felt empathy. I knew she had a new boyfriend, and I have experienced that strong desire to stay connected to your love at every possible chance. I also knew that what I think and feel matter to her, and that she appreciates my approval of her and her work. So, being that I learned to be a people-pleaser, I didn't say anything for a few minutes. In my mind, I imagined what I might say and how she might feel offended or bothered by my request—how it might create distance or awkwardness.

As we continued to talk I realized that right before me was the opportunity to practice what I am preaching…in this very chapter! So, I got up the courage to state my observation (O). "It seems like your phone has become a distraction today. When you look down at it, I look down." Before I could even get to sorting my thoughts and feelings she said, "Oh, I'm so, so sorry. I'll put it away right now," and she quickly put it into her purse. I didn't even get the chance to go through the rest—S, C, A, and R! My assistant, also a people-pleaser, anticipated how I was feeling and what I was going to ask. She spared me from having to actually share my feelings and make a request. I guess that's one benefit of attracting other emotionally sensitive, people-pleasing types. We are really good at anticipating others'

responses and sparing ourselves from awkward conversations—
and having to practice our assertiveness skills!

Now let's look at another example that illustrates all five
OSCAR steps. Latisha felt burdened by the requests of a girlfriend who struggled financially, had a number of health problems, and didn't have reliable transportation. The friend would
often ask Latisha for rides to doctors' appointments and to the
grocery store. Latisha wanted to help, but realized (O) that she
was using too much of her time and energy accommodating her
friend—and had even begun to resent her (the gift of resentment) (S). Realizing she needed to make a change, she expressed
to her friend that while she values her friendship, she could
only drive her to one appointment each week (C). Her friend
was initially upset, so Latisha asked her for her perspective (A).
Her friend expressed disappointment, sadness, and some fear
about not being able to get where she needs to go. Latisha then
made a direct request (R), "It would mean a lot to me if you
would let me know by Sunday which days and times you need
help with transportation so I can let you know which day I am
able to help. If you don't let me know by Sunday, I can't guaran-
tee that I'll be able to help you that week."

## Practice Makes "Good Enough"

As a young child I was amazed by the fact that my dad, a professional musician and composer, could play any song I requested
on the piano with his eyes closed. I marveled as he played so
smoothly and beautifully without having to look at the piano
keys or music. As I grew, he started telling stories of how he
would often stay in from recess to practice piano in elementary
school, or how, as a teenager, he'd take girls out on dates that
often included watching him practice or playing at a local gig.

Over time I was able to see the connection between my dad's seemingly effortless musical expression, even with his eyes closed, and his pattern of practicing piano up to five or six hours a day. All of that practice strengthened his neural connections over time until he got to a point where playing the piano was almost effortless.

Just like learning to play an instrument, developing new communication patterns requires not only changing your knee-jerk responses to a situation but also changing the wiring in your brain. The more you do it, the more it becomes second nature and doesn't require so much conscious effort. The more you practice the Lantern stance, the easier and more natural it will become in your interactions. Luckily, you won't have to practice the Lantern stance for five hours each day. Consciously using it a few times a week should be enough for it to feel more comfortable and to become more of a habit.

## When Your Boundaries Aren't Respected

No matter how skilled you are at setting boundaries and communicating clearly, some people will continually disregard, dismiss, and cross your boundaries. They may refuse to respect your requests. There are people with whom these assertiveness skills will not work. People who cross your boundaries in this way are usually incredibly wounded individuals who have not developed healthy boundaries of their own or secure attachments. They are also at a very low level of differentiation—they can't separate thinking and feeling; they can't distinguish their emotions and needs from others. And they are generally reactive instead of responsive. These individuals are toxic because they poison the people around them.

There are times when, for your emotional and physical well-being and safety, it's best to discontinue a relationship or to take a time-out. Breaking up or cutting ties is particularly difficult when you care deeply about the other person, when he or she has been in your life for a long time, or when you feel responsible for his or her pain.

If you have an avoidant attachment style, you may have the desire to end a relationship *too* soon. Or you might perceive that someone is disregarding your boundaries even if he is simply standing up for himself or desiring a closer relationship with you. Your style will lean more toward preventing conflict and protecting yourself from getting too close.

If you lean toward an anxious attachment style, you may be prone to hang on to a toxic relationship too long or make excuses for another person's pattern of boundary crossing for fear of being alone or for fear of losing your sense of self.

If you have a securely attached style you will be able to trust your thoughts and feelings to accurately assess when it's time to let go of a relationship for your own protection. If you're not sure if it's time to discontinue a relationship, you likely have people you trust with whom you can discuss your concerns and who will help you to decide what's in your best interest.

It is really difficult to "break up" with or put distance between a loved one who consistently disregards your boundaries. It's particularly painful when the unhealthy relationship is with someone you "should" be close to. Detaching from someone in your family can also have repercussions in other relationships. No one teaches us how to do distance from a relationship in an assertive way. Let's look at Melanie's case as an example of choosing to distance herself from a loved one after boundaries are consistently disregarded.

Melanie and her mother, Lynn, have always had a tumultuous relationship. And since Melanie got married and had children, Melanie's relationship with her mom became increasingly strained. Even though Melanie had repeatedly asked her mother not to speak poorly about Lynn's ex-husband, Chris (Melanie's father), in front of her son, Lynn continued to share inappropriate details about why she divorced Melanie's dad and why they shouldn't talk to him anymore.

In addition to saying negative things about Chris, Lynn also did and said things that, from Melanie's perspective, undermined her relationship with her son. Melanie recounted, "Last time my son came home from my mom's house, he was upset because she was saying mean things. She told him that I'm just like my dad: self-centered and with a short fuse. She talked most of the time about his two twin cousins—how they are so smart, they are so athletic, and that she has never missed one of their basketball games. He was in tears because she had only gone to *one* of his basketball games. 'Why doesn't grandma like me?' he asked me. I've had it with my mom. I've asked her for several years to stop talking trash about my dad to me or to my son. And now she's putting my son down, too. I don't know what else to do."

This was not the first time Melanie had complained about her mother. Melanie loved her mom—they'd been through a lot together—but Lynn still wasn't respecting Melanie's boundaries. Melanie decided it was time to back up her verbal requests with action; she would distance herself from her mom, see her less frequently, and no longer let her spend time with her son without Melanie present. Here's what she said to her mother on the phone: "Mom, I've requested several times that you not talk badly about my dad in front of me and my family. You continue to bring up negative things about him and I'm upset about it. Also, I've asked you at least three times before that, when you're with my son, not to say bad things about me. Last time he came home from your house he was in tears because of things that you said. Until I am confident that you can follow through with my requests, we will not be coming over for our weekly visit."

In this chapter we've talked about some concrete tools to help you set strong boundaries with compassion; to make direct and clear requests based on your thoughts, feelings, wants, and needs; how to express yourself in ways that make it more likely that your boundaries will be heard and respected; and when to let go of a relationship with someone who crosses your boundaries. In the next chapter, we'll tie the concepts together by returning to the lantern metaphor as a symbol of assertive communication.

# CHAPTER 9

# Self-Expansion:
# Holding the Lantern

Remember when we talked about the Lantern in chapter 6? We used the metaphor to describe an ideal of communicating that is consistent with a secure attachment style and a higher differentiation level (but can also be developed and practiced by individuals who lean toward either an avoidant or anxious style, and a low differentiation level). In this the final chapter, we'll use the metaphor of the lantern to tie together the concepts and skills in this book—attachment styles, differentiation, emotions, assertive communication, and potential barriers—by providing examples and scenarios of the Lantern stance. The Lantern stance integrates all of the five skills of assertiveness: self-reflection, self-awareness, self-soothing, self-expression, and self-expansion.

Now let's expand on the Lantern stance, particularly to represent the benefits or the results of practicing and integrating the five skills of assertiveness: the development of *clarity, confidence, calmness, connection,* and *compassion.*

# Self-Reflection Brings Clarity

Holding up the lantern in your relationships requires under-standing of your *own* development. The knowledge gained from self-reflection provides *clarity* about how your communication patterns developed and about your default expectations in rela-tionships. When you take clarity and understanding into your communication, you can allow the lantern's light to shine on you without fear of what you'll find out about yourself.

Through continued self-reflection and understanding of your story of development, you can have clarity about your communication style, patterns, and challenges. By understand-ing whether you developed more of an anxious, secure, or avoid-ant attachment style, hopefully you have been able to make sense of *why* you engage the way you do in your relationships at every level of relational intimacy (remember the concentric circle figure from chapter 1?). Now it makes sense why, if you're more of an anxious style, you worry so much about being liked, you often are the one who wants more closeness in relation-ships than others do, you struggle to know what you think and how you feel, you get worried when there is too much distance in your relationships, it's sometimes difficult for you to know what *you* think and feel from what *others* think and feel, and emotions easily overwhelm you. Sometimes just knowing more about what's actually going on with you can help you to calm yourself down and communicate from a place of more security.

I hope the skills of sorting thoughts and feelings, and iden-tifying and managing your emotions, have been particularly valuable to you in bringing clarity into your communication and relationships. As you practice these skills they will con-tinue to become a more natural repertoire in your communica-tion. You will be able to use them to assert your feelings, thoughts, needs, and wants.

If you assessed in earlier chapters that you're more toward the avoidant style, then it makes more sense why you back away or detach from intense emotions, and why you really like your space in relationships. You value letting things "roll off of your back." Knowing how this style developed has allowed you to understand yourself and become more tuned in to your feelings and more emotionally engaged in relationships. Hopefully, you are more aware of your feelings, thoughts, needs, and wants and are better equipped to know how you differ from those around you. Continuing to practice awareness of your internal cues will help you know *what* to assertively express to others and how to allow others to get to know you on a deeper level.

If you assessed yourself as having a secure style in the beginning of this book, then skill building is what you've likely taken from these pages. Since you probably already had a direct communication style, a higher comfort level in expressing difference, and an ability to be assertive in many situations, I hope this book has helped you to gain more clarity about your development and about which skills you need to continue to work on. Since you learned early on in life how to be comfortable being both close to others *and* to tolerate distance or disconnection, this book will hopefully have helped you to understand more about yourself and your development—and solidified your emotional management and assertive communication skills.

Speaking from experience, I have benefited greatly from practicing self-reflection, making sense of my life story, and integrating the good and bad, the joy and the pain. Understanding that I developed an anxious style and a low to moderate level of differentiation helped me to develop healthy strategies to manage my anxiety surrounding separateness. One of the things that I did as an adolescent to work toward a more secure style was to consciously do things by myself that would be uncomfortable. To be clear, this *was* a therapy assignment. I went to a movie by myself, took myself to dinner, and went skiing by myself. This was the beginning of a beautiful friendship...with me. In the thirty years since then, I have continued to practice spending time alone—and now I can't function without time alone! Reflecting on, making sense of, and creating an integrated narrative of my life history has allowed me to feel more confident in my relationships, including asserting myself.

## Self-Awareness Develops to Confidence

When I first introduced the idea of the Lantern stance, I talked about visualizing yourself with your feet firmly planted on the ground. This affords a sense of stability and *confidence* that is mirrored internally by your higher level of self-awareness. Throughout this book I've presented many ideas and skills to help you connect to your emotions, label them, and use them as information to guide your life.

Remember the feelings word list? If you are ever at a loss as to what you are feeling, that list can be a great place to begin to identify your bodily cues and sensations. We talked about the importance of emotional intelligence in chapter 5, but I didn't mention that people who develop emotional intelligence, or the ability to *think about feeling* and use it to guide action, are more likely to flourish in all areas of life! This ability to use both feelings and thoughts (wise mind) to center your responses is crucial to effective assertive communication. When you are self-aware, you can have the confidence to know your feelings, thoughts, needs, and wants, and you're more equipped to see and understand the minds of others. Dr. Dan Siegel calls this "Mindsight" (2010). You can consider yours *and* others' experiences and use that awareness to inform your responses. A broader awareness greatly increases the chance of experiencing and behaving in ways that strengthen the relationship through mutual understanding.

Now that you are able to connect to your emotions, you have the tools to distinguish a thought from a feeling (part of differentiation), identify your needs and wants, and communicate them from a place of balance (wise mind). You can remain confident in your assertive communication. This confidence also allows you to let others get emotionally close to you while at the same time allowing them to be separate from you.

After twenty-seven years of marriage, I have had many opportunities to practice self-awareness and how to clearly communicate my feelings, thoughts, needs, and wants. Early on in our marriage, our extended families hosted many events. My husband, Jeff, and I were, and still are, close to our families of origin and enjoy being with them, so sometimes there was disagreement about which celebration to attend. Since then, we have learned to identify and express our feelings, thoughts, needs, and wants regarding family events. I can say, "I'm going to sit this one out, but I totally support you going to the party." And Jeff has said things like, "It would mean a lot to me if we could celebrate the Fourth of July with my family this year because my sister and her family will be in town." We are much more tolerant of each other's differences and can more easily respect those different feelings, thoughts, needs, and wants.

## Self-Soothing Results in Calmness

The Lantern stance requires a certain level of mindfulness, or the ability to observe your internal states *and* the current interaction with curiosity, openness, and without judgment. The emotional management skills taught in this book can help you remain calm even when difficult emotions arise (and they will arise...on a regular basis...because you are in relationships... and that's just what happens). Practicing wise mind, or the integration of thoughts and feelings, and responding from a place of calm and confidence will change your communication patterns!

Although assertiveness isn't always calm or "Zen," the emotional intensity that accompanies certain situations comes from an intentional place, not a reactive place. Too often assertiveness is mistaken for getting so fed up that you blow up. That is *not* assertiveness. Assertiveness is intentional, even when it's emotionally intense.

Keeping in mind that the thread throughout all humanity is our common suffering can help you feel a lot less isolated when you are in a painful or difficult situation. Responding to yourself as kindly and compassionately as you would a loved one does wonders to calm yourself down.

I am practicing self-compassion right now, even as I type. I missed my final manuscript deadline and I'm working around the clock to finish this book. I have been disengaged with my family and friends for several days and feeling guilty about neglecting my two youngest kids (they're not really neglected, I'm just not the one caring for my children; their dad is). I am continually reassuring myself with self-talk like, "It's okay. You're okay. This is hard work. You are there for them most of the time. They know they are loved. Keep writing. You can do this. Take a break and take a hot bath, and then come back to writing. You can do this!"

The ability to assess what is fact from the meaning you are giving a scenario, or the story you are telling about it, can and will help you to remain calm and hold up your lantern. And once again, using my current situation, I am practicing this right now. The *facts* are:

- This manuscript was due two days ago.

- It wasn't complete at that time.

- I am doing what it takes to submit a finished manuscript by Monday morning at 9 a.m.

The story or meaning I had been giving to the facts was something along the lines of "I must be lazy." I started believing those negative thoughts or stories about the facts, then it put me in a state of panic and I was less able to write clearly.

## Self-Expression Enables More Connection

The goal of the Lantern stance is to facilitate healthier connections and close relationships. Human beings are designed to be *in* relationships. To be known, loved, felt, and connected. It is in relationships that we develop our first sense of self—in the eyes of our parents or caregivers we discover who we are and who we can be. As we grow in relationships, if we are open to the opportunities for growth, we are refined and we mature through the process.

Self-expression is a vital part of building connections with others because it is the way that you convey your internal experiences and become "known" by another person. Remember very early on in this book when we discussed intimacy as "into me, see," or as a question: "Will you see into me? If I share myself will you know me? Will you love me?" Your ability to self-express both in words and in behavior allows you to develop closer and more authentic connections. It also allows you to set strong boundaries when necessary to protect yourself or the rights of someone you love. It is through self-expression that you make and reinforce your assertive communication and relationship boundaries.

While holding the lantern, you are able to express difference, make requests, and balance your feelings, thoughts, needs, and wants with the perspectives of others. You now have more tools to express yourself, including what makes you *different*, which ironically allows you to be closer to others and to be known.

I have had to communicate clearly and assertively recently to create space to (you guessed it) finish this book. I have had to say to my husband, "I need six hours of uninterrupted time to write today. Will you make sure the kids get to their choir performance tonight?" On an emotional level I've expressed a range of emotions to my family members and friends. "I'm exhausted. I'm feeling insecure. I'm feeling scared that I'm not good enough or strong enough." My ability to express vulnerability and my family's willingness to respond with empathy has strengthened our connection.

## Self-Expansion Grows Compassion

When you are standing firmly with your feet squarely apart, holding up the lantern, you not only see the situation at hand more clearly, but the lantern's light allows you to be more aware of others' suffering and how you might help. This is self-expansion—an awareness of others' experiences, a willingness to feel *with* them, to be changed by them, and be moved by them in a way that inspires you to do something to ease *their* pain.

You'll recall that we talked about self-compassion as practice for self-soothing and emotional management in chapter 6, and the importance of empathy in chapters 5 and 8. So, what's the difference between compassion and empathy? They are related, like cousins, but they are not identical twins.

Compassion is the ability to "feel with another" (similar to empathy) combined with the desire to take *action* and to alleviate the suffering. The difference between empathy and compassion is that compassion includes a desire to *act* in a way that lightens the burden of another person.

The longer you hold the lantern, the more connected you become to your own experience, to those with whom you're relating, and you begin to expand your view and shine the light wider and wider and wider...

I've experienced this self-expansion most acutely by being a parent. Parenting is surely not the only relationship where you can experience self-expansion, but it has significantly expanded me in dramatic ways. When I was expecting our second child I was afraid. I was fearful because I knew there was no way on earth I could love another child the way I loved our first child, Tanner. It didn't seem possible. Maybe I could love another child almost as much, but not that much.

Our second child, Madeline, was born a week before Christmas and the labor was...well...intense. After she was born I held Madeline against my chest and my fear melted away. I could, and I did, love another child as much as I loved Tanner. That is the beauty of relationships and of loving—it multiplies and expands our capacities, it expands our hearts and our minds.

My birthing experience offered an opportunity for self-expansion, as did the opportunity to witness a loved one facing mortality. My father-in-law passed away eight years ago from stomach cancer. He was able to spend his final weeks and days at home. People from all chapters of his life came to say goodbye and to thank him for his positive influence in their lives. No one mentioned his professional accomplishments, his service in the army, his bank account, or the kind of car he used to drive. The only thing that was expressed was love, and the only things that mattered in his final days were his relationships—his cherished connections with family and friends. In his final moments of life, as he lay in his own bed, with his wife next to him and his family surrounding him, there was *only love*.

It is in the entrances and exits of life that the meaning and purpose of living comes into focus. Life's purpose is to connect deeply with each other and to learn how to love.

# Acknowledgments

This book represents a culmination of two decades of professional experience as a licensed clinical social worker and psychotherapist, along with more than four decades of life experience—it's hard to know where to begin expressing gratitude! So I'll just start at the beginning.

Thank you to my heavenly parents for sending me to this "life school," and to my Redeemer for being a "lamp unto my feet" and affording me the opportunity to grow through mistakes and missteps. Thank you to my mom, Linda de Azevedo, and my dad, Lex de Azevedo, for fostering a "family laboratory" where authentic expression, big dreams, mission-driven creativity, and lasting family connections could flourish, and where faith, forgiveness, and love could be practiced and refined. I cannot imagine life without my eight freaking-amazing siblings and their families: Carrie de Azevedo Poulsen, Emilie de Azevedo Brown, Lex de Azevedo, Rachel de Azevedo Coleman,

Rebecca de Azevedo Overson, Christian de Azevedo, Sarah de Azevedo, and Aaron de Azevedo. Thank you for your love, support, life-long friendship, and your inspiring efforts to transform the world.

The support of my family has been invaluable in the process of writing this book. It could not have come to fruition without the practical support and lasting love of my husband, Jeff, and my children: Tanner and Anna Hanks, Madeline, Owen, and Macy. It is through our relationships that I have found the most "growth opportunities" and the most joy.

Thank you to my professors, teachers, and professional mentors for seeing the potential I possessed when I couldn't see it, particularly Justin Moore and Jocelyn Chapman. I am indebted to my mentor and dear friend Margaret Thompson for introducing me to psychodynamic theories and attachment theory, and for helping me to integrate it into my clinical work and into my life.

Unfortunately, this next group I want to acknowledge can't be referenced by name (but you know who you are). I am deeply indebted to my clients through the years for sharing your stories and the most tender parts of your life's journey with me. It is an honor to be welcomed into your hearts and your lives, and I hold our experiences very sacred. Thank you for showing me the beauty of our common humanity, for helping me see myself more clearly, and for trusting me to walk with you in your darkest times.

One of the benefits of owning my own practice is that I get to choose who will join my professional family at Wasatch Family Therapy. The camaraderie, authenticity, laughter, and clinical skill that you demonstrate inspire me. Thank you Monette, Michael, Ashley, Rachel, Amy, Tyler, LaShawn,

Kathleen, Kelly, Samantha, Jameson, Haylee, Holly, and all past team members for your enduring friendship, professional consultation, and ongoing support. Special thanks to Clair Mellenthin, my right-hand woman, clinical twin, trusted friend. I want to acknowledge the amazing work of my office manager/administrative assistant and "left brain," Brittany Wimer. I couldn't have completed this book without knowing that you're taking care of all of the clinic details.

To my dear friends Jennie, Wendy, Jamie, Rene, and Christi for your love and support and sustaining friendship.

Much gratitude to Katherine Wilkinson, my writing assistant, for helping refine the concepts in this book, for your thoughtful input, and for tirelessly working to keep this project moving forward. I couldn't have completed this book without your dedication and support.

I am honored to work with New Harbinger Publications, and I'm grateful for the opportunity to publish a book on a topic I feel very strongly about—empowering women to find and use their authentic voice in their lives, relationships, and in the world. Thank you to the NH team—particularly Angela, Jess, Melissa, Jesse, and Nicola—for ongoing support and feedback throughout the writing and editing process. To Marisa Solís, my dream copy editor: Thank you for working your magic and smoothing the rough edges of this book with sensitivity and grace.

I am indebted to my heroine, Riane Eisler. Your dominator/partnership continuum is now integrated into my being, my worldview, my personal and professional work, and in my everyday conversations. That you would agree to write this book's foreword is a tremendous honor.

And thank you *you* for reading this book and for valuing my voice.

# Recommended Reading

Alberti, Robert E., and Michael L. Emmons. 1982. *Your Perfect Right: A Guide to Assertive Living*. San Luis Obispo, CA: Impact Publishers.

Brown, C. Brené. 2010. *The Gifts of Imperfection: Let Go of Who You Think You're Supposed to Be and Embrace Who You Are*. Center City, MN: Hazelden.

Brown, Brené. 2012. *Daring Greatly: How the Courage to Be Vulnerable Transforms the Way We Live, Love, Parent, and Lead*. New York: Gotham Books.

Cloud, Henry, and John Sims Townsend. 1992. *Boundaries: When to Say Yes, When to Say No to Take Control of Your Life*. Grand Rapids, MI: Zondervan Publishing House.

Davis, Martha, Elizabeth Robbins Eshelman, and Matthew McKay. 2008. *The Relaxation and Stress Reduction Workbook*. Oakland, CA: New Harbinger Publications.

Fensterheim, Herbert, and Jean L. Baer. 1975. *Don't Say Yes When You Want to Say No: How Assertiveness Training Can Change Your Life*. New York: McKay.

Goleman, Daniel. 1995. *Emotional Intelligence*. New York: Bantam Books.

Hanson, Rick. 2011. *Just One Thing: Developing a Buddha Brain One Simple Practice at a Time*. Oakland, CA: New Harbinger Publications.

McKay, Matthew, Jeffrey C. Wood, and Jeffrey Brantley. 2007. *The Dialectical Behavior Therapy Skills Workbook: Practical DBT Exercises for Learning Mindfulness, Interpersonal Effectiveness, Emotion Regulation, and Distress Tolerance*. Oakland, CA: New Harbinger Publications.

McKay, Matthew, Patrick Fanning, and Patricia Zurita Ona. 2011. *Mind and Emotions: A Universal Treatment for Emotional Disorders*. Oakland, CA: New Harbinger Publications.

Neff, Kristin. 2011. *Self-Compassion: Stop Beating Yourself Up and Leave Insecurity Behind*. NY: HarperCollins.

Paterson, Randy J. 2000. *The Assertiveness Workbook: How to Express Your Ideas and Stand Up for Yourself at Work and in Relationships*. Oakland, CA: New Harbinger Publications.

Schnarch, David Morris. 2012. *Passionate Marriage: Keeping Love and Intimacy Alive in Committed Relationships*. Brunswick, Vic: Scribe Publications.

Siegel, Daniel J. 2010. *Mindsight: The New Science of Personal Transformation*. New York: Bantam Books.

Siegel, Judith P. 2010. *Stop Overreacting: Effective Strategies for Calming Your Emotions*. Oakland, CA: New Harbinger Publications.

# References

Ainsworth, Mary S. 1979. "Infant-Mother Attachment." *American Psychologist* 34 (10): 932–937.

Bowen, Murray. 1976. "Theory in the Practice of Psychotherapy." In P. J. Guerin Jr. (Ed.), *Family Therapy: Theory and Practice* (pp. 42–90). New York: Garner Press.

Bowlby, John. 1958. "The Nature of the Child's Tie to His Mother." *The International Journal of Psycho-Analysis* 39: 350–379.

Brown, Brené. 2012. *Daring Greatly: How the Courage to be Vulnerable Transforms the Way We Live, Love, Parent, and Lead.* New York: Gotham.

Coltrane, Scott, and Michele Adams. 2008. *Gender and Families.* Lanham, MD: Rowman & Littlefield Publishers.

Eisenberger, Naomi I. 2015. "Social Pain and the Brain: Controversies, Questions, and Where to Go from Here." *Annual Review of Psychology* 66 (1): 601–629.

Eisler, Riane Tennenhaus. 1987. *The Chalice and the Blade: Our History, Our Future.* Cambridge, MA: Harper & Row.

Etaugh, Claire, and Judith S. Bridges. 2015. *Women's Lives: A Psychological Exploration.* New York: Psychology Press.

Ferguson, Tamara J., Heidi L. Eyre, and Michael Ashbaker. 2000. "Unwanted Identities: A Key Variable in Shame-Anger Links and Gender Differences in Shame." *Sex Roles* 42 (3/4): 133–157.

George, C., N. Kaplan, and M. Main. 1985. *The Adult Attachment Interview.* Unpublished manuscript, University of California at Berkeley.

Gilligan, Carol. 1982. *In a Different Voice: Psychological Theory and Women's Development.* Cambridge, MA: Harvard University Press.

Gottman, John M., and J. DeClaire. 1992. *Raising an Emotionally Intelligent Child: The Heart of Parenting.* Upper Saddle River, NJ: Prentice Hall.

Gottman, John Mordechai, Nan Silver, and John Allen Nelson. 1999. *The Seven Principles for Making Marriage Work.* Old Saybrook, CT: Tantor Media, Inc.

Hanks, Julie de Azevedo. 2013. *The Burnout Cure: An Emotional Survival Guide for Overwhelmed Women.* American Fork, UT: Covenant.

Hanks, Julie de Azevedo. 2015. "(Pro)creating: Transforming Constraints to Creative Productivity of Mothers Through a Partnership Model of Family Organization." Doctoral dissertation. **http://search.proquest.com/docview/1686128354**.

Hazan, C., and P. Shaver. 1987. "Romantic Love Conceptualized as an Attachment Process." Journal of Personality and Social Psychology 52 (3): 511–24.

Johnson, Sue. 2008. *Hold Me Tight: Seven Conversations for a Lifetime of Love*. New York: Little, Brown & Co.

Johnson, Sue. 2013. *Love Sense: The Revolutionary New Science of Romantic Relationships*. New York: Little, Brown & Co.

Kabat-Zinn, Jon. 1994. *Wherever You Go There You Are: Mindfulness Meditation in Everyday Life*. New York: Hyperion.

Katie, Byron, and Stephen Mitchell. 2002. *Loving What Is*. San Bruno, CA: Audio Literature.

Kernis, Michael H. 2005. "Measuring Self-Esteem in Context: The Importance of Stability of Self-Esteem in Psychological Functioning." *Journal of Personality* 73 (6): 1,569–1,605.

Kuhn, Maggie, Christina Long, and Laura Quinn. 1991. *No Stone Unturned: The Life and Times of Maggie Kuhn*. New York: Ballantine.

Linehan, Marsha. 1993. *Skills Training Manual for Treating Borderline Personality Disorder*. New York: Guilford Press.

Meyer, M. L., K. D. Williams, and N. I. Eisenberger. 2015. "Why Social Pain Can Live On: Different Neural Mechanisms Are Associated with Reliving Social and Physical Pain." *PLoS ONE* 10(6). eScholarship, University of California. http://www.escholarship.org/uc/item/6pt8b9m6. http://dx.doi.org/10.1371%2Fjournal.pone.0128294

Miller, Jean Baker. 1987. *Toward a New Psychology of Women*. 2nd ed. Boston: Beacon.

Miller, Jean Baker, and Irene P. Stiver. 1997. *The Healing Connection: How Women Form Relationships in Therapy and in Life*. Boston: Beacon Press.

Murakami, Haruki, and Philip Gabriel. 2008. *What I Talk About When I Talk About Running: A Memoir.* New York: Alfred A. Knopf.

Neff, Kristin. 2003. "Self-Compassion: An Alternative Conceptualization of a Healthy Attitude Toward Oneself." *Self and Identity* 2 (2): 85–101.

Neff, Kristin. 2011. *Self-Compassion: Stop Beating Yourself Up and Leave Insecurity Behind.* New York: William Morrow/HarperCollins.

Neff, Kristin D., and R. Vonk. 2009. "Self-Compassion versus Global Self-Esteem: Two Different Ways of Relating to Oneself." *Journal of Personality* 77 (1): 23–50. doi:10.1111/j.1467–6494.2008.00537.x.

Pipher, Mary. 1994. *Reviving Ophelia: Saving the Selves of Adolescent Girls.* New York: Ballantine Books.

Salovey, P., and J. D. Mayer. 1990. "Emotional Intelligence." *Imagination, Cognition, and Personality* 9: 185–211.

Sapolsky, Robert M. 2004. *Why Zebras Don't Get Ulcers.* New York: Times Books.

Schnarch, David Morris. 1997. *Passionate Marriage: Love, Sex, and Intimacy in Emotionally Committed Relationships.* New York: W. W. Norton.

Siegel, Daniel J. 2010. *Mindsight: The New Science of Personal Transformation.* New York: Bantam Books.

Watzlawick, P., J. H. Beavin, and D. D. Jackson. 1967. *Pragmatics of Human Communication: A Study of Interactional Patterns, Pathologies, and Paradoxes.* New York: Norton.

Wiseman, T. 1996. "A Concept Analysis of Empathy." *Journal of Advanced Nursing* 23 (6): 1,162–7.

**Julie de Azevedo Hanks, PhD, LCSW,** is passionate about helping women find their voice in their own lives, relationships, and in the world. She is a psychotherapist and licensed clinical social worker, author of *The Burnout Cure*, blogger, local and national media contributor, online influencer, consultant, award-winning performing songwriter, and founder and director of Wasatch Family Therapy. A native Californian, Hanks currently lives in Salt Lake City, UT, with her husband and their four children. For more information, visit **www.drjulie hanks.com**.

Foreword writer **Riane Eisler, JD,** is a systems scientist, cultural historian, author of *The Chalice and the Blade* and *The Real Wealth of Nations*, and coauthor of *Transforming Interprofessional Partnerships*. She has been a leader in the movement for peace, sustainability, and economic equity, and her pioneering work in human rights has expanded the focus of international organizations to include the rights of women and children. For more information, visit **www.rianeeisler.com**.